LIVING LOVE PUBLISHERS

PRESENTS

I0181299

Suicide Is Not Your Answer

Patricia Dascher

Printed in the United States of America

First Printing, 2017

ISBN-10: 0-9974874-1-0

ISBN-13: 978-0-9974874-1-1

Soul Magazine, Inc.
PO Box 216
Sunrise Beach, MO 65079

www.PatriciaDascher.com

www.SoulMagazine.org

Table of Contents

Appreciation

My sincere thanks go to my husband, Dr. Richard Dascher, who has supported, encouraged and helped me in writing this book. To my daughter Kimberly Love, who has provided the wisdom and knowledge to put this book online and assisted in getting this book to you.

Dedication

This book is dedicated to all who have been suicidal. And to those who have loved ones who are suicidal or have lost a loved one to suicide.

Introduction

I was 23 when I stood in a graveyard thinking, "The only people who have peace are those in these graves."

Suicide was not my answer, and it is not YOUR answer. A whispered prayer over 40 years ago changed my life from despair to love, joy, and peace.

Suicide has touched the lives of multitudes around the world. Because I chose life, God was able to use me to help others choose life.

"I'm a "nothin' " and a nobody, and it doesn't matter what happens to me anyway," said Michael, a 15-year-old boy who lived in a juvenile court facility.

"God doesn't make nothin's, and nobody's," I told him.

Michael and all those I worked with over the years chose life. This book will show you how to encourage and help those in need. It will let you know when they need to go to the hospital and when they need encouragement to keep going.

"I know the plans I have for you," declares the LORD, "plans to prosper you and not to harm you, plans to give you hope and a future. ¹² Then you will call on me and come and pray to me, and I will listen to you. ¹³ You will seek me and find me when you seek me with all your heart." (Jeremiah 29:11-13 New International Version (NIV))

2

God has a plan for good, not evil. To give us a future and a hope. God shows us the way. He doesn't waste a tear.

No matter how dark life seems, there is a light just behind the clouds of despair. The light of God's love still shines. It is there whether we see and feel it or not.

This book will take you through a juvenile court facility where multitudes of children and youth are sent. It is a place where many feel angry, depressed and sometimes suicidal. It will show the despair of women in a battered women's shelter. A hospital's psychiatric ward filled with youth who have attempted suicide. A prison filled with ladies who needed inner healing. Those in the military and their families who faced post-traumatic stress disorder causing more to die from suicide than in combat. The book talks about Borderline Personality, Bi-Polar, sexual abuse in childhood and much more.

God has a plan for each of our lives. We are His gift to the world. He can take our disastrous mistakes and turn them into blessings. He is bigger than our failures, mistakes, and sins. His light shines through the darkest depression when we let Him lead us.

The stories I have shared throughout this book are true; but many of the names, places, and organizations have been changed to protect the confidentiality of those I write about.

;

Project Semicolon

Life and death battles are going on today with depression, anxiety, self-injury, post-traumatic stress disorder and suicide. Like most battles if we don't know the enemy or how to fight back we lose the fight. Our young people are coming out today with a symbol that says, "I'm in this battle for my life, but I am not giving up. My life isn't over."

The symbol of the "**semicolon**" is to let others know they have chosen not to end the sentence of their lives. Project Semicolon is a global faith-based not for profit movement to give hope and love to those struggling with self-injury, depression, suicide or addictions.

If you see someone with the symbol of a "semicolon," let them know you care and that their life is valuable. More information about this semicolon project can be found at the following sites;

www.the-semicolon-movement.tumblr.com

www.projectsemicolon.org

4

1

Inner Healing for Ladies in Prison

Volunteering at a Correctional Institute

"The inmates get tired of people preaching on what they are doing wrong," the administrator of the minimum risk prison told me.

"Let me come a few times to conduct 'Inner Healing' groups," I said. "If they aren't interested, I will stop coming."

"You aren't going to find them very receptive, but if you want to try, go ahead."

I was scheduled to come in at 10 am on a Thursday morning. Thirty women shuffled over to a group session on my first visit. The minimum risk prison facility had what looked like cots the ladies slept on in one big room. The women were still wearing their bathrobes and fluffy slippers. Some had rollers in their hair. The security guard warned me about a tiny young woman with scars all over her face and arms. "Do you see that lady? She is the meanest thing we have ever had in here. Her name is Jodie. Watch out for her."

5

"Another freeway 'do-gooder' that thinks she can tell us how to live," I heard an inmate say to the guard.

The ladies yawned and acted annoyed for being forced to come to the group. I realized my pink suit and heels were the wrong outfit to wear to the prison. I should have worn a sweatshirt and jeans, but it was too late.

I knew unless God helped me, there was nothing I could say to help them. "Show me what to say, Lord," I prayed.

My Testimony To The Inmates

"I was in prison once," I said. "It wasn't a prison with guards, bars, and locks as it is here. My prison was depression, despair, hopelessness, and suicide."

I suddenly had the undivided attention of all the ladies. "At the age of 13, I decided suicide was my only way out of a life filled with abuse. I was never rocked or held. No one ever said, "I love you."

At birth, I was left at the hospital to be taken in by a foster family. My parents were penniless and could not afford another child. I was a baby boomer born the day after Christmas but was not considered a gift by my parents. They struggled financially and were kicked out of their apartment right after I was born. My father had been out of work for months.

After being with my foster mother for a year, she tried to adopt me. My father said, "She wasn't supposed to fall in

6

love with you. Your grandmother and I couldn't let her have you.

I went back to my birth family when my mother was pregnant with my brother. She was angry at having to care for another child. She continually slapped and beat me calling me filthy names. She blamed me for all her frustrations telling my father what a bad child I was and how tired she was of taking care of me. My mother often slapped me in the face giving me a bloody nose for talking. She went into violent rages calling me a tramp, slut or whore long before I knew what those words meant. She often said, "I wish you had never been born."

At the age of thirteen both my parents came to me saying, "We are going to talk to your grandmother about your living with her. You don't get along with your mother."

The feeling of being unwanted by my family filled me with grief. My grandmother said she could not take me because she worked full time and her husband was an alcoholic. I stood at the hall closet of my childhood home with a bottle of aspirin in my hand. "I can't take it anymore," I told God as I filled my hand with aspirin.

In my mind I heard these words, "Can you make it three more years? I will get you out of here in three years."

"I guess I could make it three more years if you help me," I answered.

I put the pills back in the bottle knowing God had spoken to me. It was not through my ears but in my heart and mind. For the next three years, I came home from school to cook, clean and help take care of my baby brother. I babysat and fixed neighbors hair. I really struggled as a student and was unable to read above a second-grade level, so I saw myself as dumb. My mother was usually lying on the couch sleeping when I got home from school. She continued to be angry and filled with rage. But I had changed. I had hope.

At 16 I was allowed to date a young college student. I got pregnant and married. I had a beautiful baby girl. I remember holding her and praying, "God, I didn't know a love like this existed."

Everyone said the marriage would not last, but I was determined to make it work. I helped my husband get through college by babysitting. I worked hard to have a good marriage, but after six years we were in the middle of a divorce.

Feeling unloved, depressed and hopeless I stood at a graveyard planning my suicide. Looking at the graves, I thought, "The only people who have peace are in their graves."

I decided I would go home and take a bottle of pills to end my life. I felt unloved and unwanted.

As I started to get into my car to leave, I looked up at the sky and saw rays of sun shining through the clouds. "Only

God can paint a picture like that," I thought. "God if you are there and care about me, would you help me?"

"Seek, and you will find. Knock, and the doors will be open to you. Ask, and it shall be given to you."

"I don't think like that," I thought to myself. "It must be God talking to me."

"I don't know what doors to knock on," I told God. "I don't know where to seek. So I ask you to send whatever it is I need to my front door."

The next morning a station wagon full of church ladies pulled up in my driveway. When I opened my front door, they said, "We have come to tell you that Jesus loves you. If you give your life to Him, He will fill you with love, joy, and peace."

I listened as the ladies told me of the love of Jesus. They encouraged me to give my life to Him. Although I had not been raised in a Christian home, I believed in Jesus and had been baptized at a local church when I was nine years old. But I knew I would fail Him. I looked at the ladies with their out of style clothes, hair, and no make-up, "I could never live up to His standards," I said as I smoked my Virginia Slims.

"Give your life to Him, and He will fill you with His Holy Spirit. He will help you do whatever He wants you to do," they told me.

That night alone in my living room I meditated on what they had said. "God, I am afraid if I give my life to you I'll have to go to Africa."

"I will never ask you to do anything I won't give you the power of my Holy Spirit to do it," He said.

"But what if you ask me to get up in front of a bunch of people and speak? I could never do that."

"I will never ask you to do anything I won't give the power of my Holy Spirit to do."

"What if you ask me to be one of those Jesus Freaks?"

"You can give your life to Me, and I will make you into a beautiful woman. Or you can keep your life and go straight to the gutter."

At first, I was offended, but then I thought, He is right. There is nothing lower than suicide. "Yes, God! You call the shots from now on," I said to Him.

I gave my life to God asking Him to do whatever He wanted to do with me. I began a journey of emotional healing. I started talking to Him all the time.

I had always wanted a man who would love me enough to die for me. I found that kind of love in Jesus who died on a bloody cross to have a relationship with me. I told Him I had never been rocked, held or loved and asked Him to rock me. When I went to sleep at night, I felt His presence rocking me saying, "*I love you with an everlasting love.*"

I looked around the room at each of the ladies. "God has sent me here to tell you He loves you. Jesus wants you to give your life to Him. You are His princess and child. I know what it is like to give your heart to someone that bounces it all over the cement spattering your soul into a million pieces. But I can promise you this. When you give your life to Jesus Christ, He will love you with an everlasting love."

Jodie started walking toward me with tears pouring down her face. "Would Jesus rock me? Does He care about me?" she asked.

She pulled up the sleeves of her shirt and showed me scars her parents had left on her from a childhood of extreme physical abuse. "They beat me and tied me up in the basement for days," she said. "No one has ever loved me. Could Jesus love someone like me?"

I wrapped my arms around her and rocked back and forth as I would a child. "Lord Jesus," I prayed out loud, "You see this broken little girl. She needs to know that you love her. I am asking you to wrap your love around her soul and rock her. Let her feel your presence and love. Heal all the broken places in her life."

As I looked up, I saw every woman in the circle rocking back and forth with their eyes filled with tears. The Holy Spirit healed the souls of thirty brokenhearted women that day. "*I came to heal the brokenhearted and set the captive free,*" Jesus said. (Luke 4:18)

Women Transformed Through the Love of God

I was amazed at the transformation of the women in the little time I was with them. When I came in on Thursday morning, they were dressed looking forward to our times together. Some of the staff started coming to share what Jesus had done for them. The words from the Bible filled their hearts with hope, love, and power. We looked at what caused them to get involved with pimps, criminals, and abusers. They learned that they did not need the love of cruel people to be happy or to cover their pain.

The atmosphere of the prison and physical appearance of the women changed as their souls were healed and they saw the beauty within themselves. They put on make-up, fixed their hair and showed me their journals. They were on a journey of inner healing as they admitted their need for God. The cycle of abuse and victimization was overcome by the power of the Holy Spirit within them.

Give your past, present, and future to God! Think about what is good! The Apostle Paul was in prison and in chains when he wrote Philippians 4:4-8 *"Always be full of joy in the Lord. I say it again—rejoice! Don't worry about anything; instead, pray about everything. Tell God what you need, and thank him for all he has done. Then you will experience God's peace, which exceeds anything we can understand. His peace will guard your hearts and minds as you live in Christ Jesus. Fix your thoughts on what is true, and honorable, and right, and pure, and lovely, and admirable. Think about things that are excellent and worthy of praise. Then the God of peace will be with you."*

2

Suicide at a Juvenile Court Facility

A Request for Our Court to Train Workers in Suicide Prevention

"It is not uncommon for our youth to talk about killing themselves. This concerns me," I said during a staff meeting at the juvenile court facility where I worked. "We need to have Suicide Prevention Classes."

"The kids talk about suicide to get attention," the staff mocked. "Patricia, you aren't streetwise. You don't understand these kids."

Timmy, 13, committed suicide two weeks after that staff meeting. A few days after Timmy was placed in our minimum risk court facility he got upset with one of the boys and started a fight. The Youth Worker yelled at him and sent him to his room after threatening to put him in detention. He ran upstairs, closed the door to his room, opened a drawer to block anyone from getting in and hung himself with the cords to the window blinds. By the time one of the workers discovered what happened, Timmy was dead.

He was upset that his mother had gotten remarried soon after his parent's divorce. He had hoped his mother and father would get back together. The court's Crisis Intervention Counselor suggested Timmy be placed in a low-risk court facility to give him time to process his anger. The counselor felt he needed to be taught a lesson about his negative attitude at home and school.

Timmy was experiencing three crisis situations at once. His mother and father got a divorce. His mother got remarried. Then he was put in a juvenile court facility where he felt fear, rejection, and abandonment.

The workers had no training or sensitivity in how to work with children in crisis. They saw their jobs as managing and controlling the youth. The Youth Workers were not trained and educated in how to help troubled youth. They had no instruction in suicide prevention, first aid or CPR. Timmy had not broken the law, yet he was treated like a criminal. He wasn't truant from school or a runaway. He was in grief over his parent's divorce and mother's remarriage. "The counselor said it would help him to be placed in the facility," his mother cried.

It took the life of a 13-year-old boy for the court to take suicide seriously. The entire system was changed because of one traumatized boy's spontaneous decision to end his life. After his death, it became mandatory for all 350 court employees to take suicide prevention classes. Staff members who worked directly with youth were also required to take CPR and First Aid, classes. From then on if a client talked about or attempted suicide they were put on "Suicide Watch."

The Children of the Juvenile Court

I worked as a night youth worker while I went to school to get a degree in Social Work. I was overwhelmed by the emotional pain I saw in most of the girls and boys living in court facilities. At one point I took a group of young people to a camping resort where there was swimming, miniature golf, boating, fishing, campfires and other activities. I was doing research on, "What Is Joy?" I asked my youngest daughter, age eight when the last time she felt joy was. She said,"I have joy every day."

When I asked the girls from the juvenile court the same question, they said things like; "I haven't had joy since my stepfather tried to flush my head down the toilet." "I have never felt joy." "I don't know what it feels like to have joy." "I haven't had joy since my mother's boyfriend raped me."

Samantha, 13, Tries to Hang Herself

Samantha attempted to hang herself with a shower curtain one evening before I arrived for my 10 pm shift. At 13, she was already 5'8", with long blond hair and big brown eyes. The youth worker on duty, Ms. Bull was raging mad. "If I were as stupid as you are I would kill myself too. Ugly, stupid girl! What were you thinking?"

Although the workers had been trained in suicide prevention and were not allowed to hit a child, many were extremely verbally abusive. The child was sobbing. "Would you mind if I had a talk with her while you do your reports?" I asked in a calm voice, "I know this has been a stressful evening for you."

"Working with stupid fools like Samantha, I'm gonna end up in a psych ward. I'm getting out of this crazy place as soon as this report is done," she yelled.

The facility held 14 minimum risk girls, 11-17, who were considered status offenders. They had never broken the law but had family problems, were truant from school or runaways.

I took Samantha into the living room where it was quiet. Her hair was stringy and hung around her face, covering her swollen red eyes. I spoke in a low voice so Ms. Bull would not hear or interfere with the hope and healing I sought to bring her. "Sweetheart," I said, "you know I care and you can talk to me."

Samantha put her face in her hands and began to sob, "I can't take it anymore Ms. Patricia. I have no reason to live. I am ugly, fat and stupid. I hate myself and my life."

I gave Samantha a piece of paper and drew a line down the middle. "I want you to write down ten things you like about yourself and ten things you would like to improve on," I said.

I went to the office as Ms. Bull finished her reports. "Thank you for taking her off my hands. These kids are going to give me a nervous breakdown," she said, "I am out of here."

I learned early in my work in the court that to say anything negative to a co-worker like Ms. Bull would only create more rage. She was an extremely obese, angry woman in her 30's. She dressed in big t-shirts and jeans. I tried to treat her with respect but prayed she would get another job because she didn't like the girls or her job.

Samantha Finds a Reason to Live

I could see Samantha writing intently from the office. A few minutes later I walked into the living area and looked at the paper. She had written ten faults but nothing positive. Her writing, spelling, and punctuation were perfect. "Samantha, you have written all you think are your faults. Could you tell me something good about yourself?"

"I can't think of anything good," she said.

"Samantha, your writing, and spelling are perfect," I said.

"They are?" she asked.

"Yes, you are a smart, attractive young lady," I said. "Could you tell me why you are in here?"

"I quit going to school," she said.

"What was keeping you from going to school?" I asked.

"I didn't want to go. I don't see any reason to go to school if I am going to be nothing but a waitress."

"Do you want to be a waitress?" I asked. I knew her parents had lost their business, so I asked her to tell me about what was going on at home.

"My parents are great. They used to own a craft store, and both of them worked a lot. We all saved to get the store. They had to close it when a big chain store moved in. I don't want to put all my hopes and dreams into something that fails. Now my dad works at that chain store. I just want to be a waitress, earn some money, go home and watch television."

"What gives you joy Samantha.

"Nothing," she said.

"What would you do all day long if you could do anything you wanted?" I asked.

"I'd have my own horse and ride it every day."

"Do you realize Sam, that there are many jobs available where you can work with horses. At the age of 13 if you begin preparing to get a job working horses you could be a great asset to stable owners who board and own them."

"Really," she said. "What kind of jobs?"

"Places that board horses are always looking for people to help care for them. If you want to be a vet that specializes in horses or an assistant, that is also possible. Anything is possible if you put your mind to it," I told her.

The next day I had a long talk with Samantha's parents. I explained that she was feeling the grief and loss of their business closing. Her way of dealing with it was not to have hopes or dreams of her own. "But there is one thing she loves," I said, "horses."

"We know that," her parents said. "But how will that help her go to school or get out of this depression?"

"I would encourage you to keep her focused on what she can do in the area she loves. Do research with her on jobs she could get working with horses. Keep her focused on a goal to do what she actually enjoys doing. It could inspire her to go to school. As she watched you lose the business, she lost her desire to work for anything, thinking it could all be taken away," I told them.

Samantha left with her parents that day with a new vision for her future. She did not return to the court.

Young teens often reflect what their parents are going through. When Samantha's parents lost their business, she lost hope as well. Youth who have lost a parent through death or divorce are also at risk. By listening, caring and inspiring, we can help our young people to find healing and hope.

Patrick, 15: "I'm a Nothin' and a Nobody."

Patrick; was a tall, slim 15-year-old with a great smile and sense of humor. He loved to tease, laugh, joke and make others laugh. Working in a minimum risk facility with 14 boys ages 7-17 was challenging and fun for me. I worked nights where I assisted in putting them to bed and fixing their breakfast. Patrick often went around waking the other kids up at 2 or 3 in the morning. I asked him to come downstairs and help me fix breakfast for the residents rather than waking them up. He was intelligent, winning all our spelling contests and athletic, excelling in basketball. He was also good at drawing cartoon characters. Rather than waking up the other residents in the middle of the night, he began helping me in the kitchen saying, "Ms. Patricia, you are the only one in the world I would bust suds for a 3 o'clock in the morning."

His mother came to see him one evening at the facility. She screamed and raged calling Patrick vile names, cursing and saying he was good for nothing. I was a new worker at the time and was shocked they allowed anyone to treat a youth in such a hateful manner.

The boys made fun of Patrick's mother after she left because she was extremely obese. Patrick told a boy to shut up and was getting ready to hit him when Ms. Riley, another worker, yelled, "You are going to end up in prison if you keep starting fights. Go to your room."

He ran up to his room holding back tears of hurt and rage. I went up to talk to him. He was lying face down on his bed crying, "I'm a nothin' and a nobody, and it doesn't matter what happens to me anyway."

"That is not true," I said firmly. "God made you, and you are special. God doesn't make nothings and nobodies. You are the smartest kid in this place. You are creative and a great artist. You are athletic and great at basketball. You are special. God made you, and He has a great purpose for your life."

I started singing a little song to him: "You're something special. You're the only one of your kind. God gave you a body and a bright, healthy mind. He has a special purpose, He wants you to find. That's why you are something special. You are the only one of your kind."

He got up, looked at me with big brown tear-filled eyes and said, "Thank you, Ms. Patricia. Thank you. I know you are right."

Patrick's mother rejected him because her boyfriend didn't want him around. The court was able to find his father, who was in the military in Germany. He wanted Patrick to be with him. Before he left to live with his father, he wrote me a note saying, "I used to think I was a nothin' and a nobody until this lady Ms. Patricia told me I was somebody special and that God loved me. I haven't felt the same since."

Attention Deficit /Hyperactivity Disorder

Working with younger boys in a minimum risk facility I found that half of them were on medication for hyperactivity. I enjoyed working with them. But they were definitely hyperactive.

High-Risk Youth

Suicide is the second leading cause of death in the youth of ages 10 to 24. More teens die from suicide than from cancer, heart disease, AIDS, birth defects, stroke, pneumonia, influenza, and chronic lung disease combined. Over 5,400 children attempt suicide every day.

Young people who have been placed in juvenile court facilities are at high risk for suicide. The following are some of the signs to look for with youth who may be dealing with depression and suicidal thoughts.
- Victim or witness of violence.
- Attention deficit hyperactivity disorder.
- Learning disability.
- Negative self-esteem.
- A Victim of Physical or sexual abuse.
- Stressful life events.
- Academic problems.
- Family conflict and relationship difficulties.
- Involvement with the juvenile justice system.
- Sensitivity to rejection or failure.
- Early childhood trauma.

The youth at a juvenile court facility need people who will listen and care. It takes just one person in the life of a troubled young person to bring healing from the past and hope for the future.

3

Suicidal Teens in the Psychiatric Ward of a Hospital

Robby Angry at the World—Quits Talking

Robby was 12 years old when he was placed in the psychiatric ward of the hospital after several suicide attempts. He was a short blond haired boy who refused to talk to anyone and was filled with anger. I met with him three times a week to do play therapy or anything that would get him out of his shell. I gave him some clay, and he made a volcano. I gave him some chalk to write on the chalkboard, and he pounded it on the board. When I asked questions or tried to talk to him, he didn't answer or would grunt. After about six meetings, I was ready to give up when I asked, "Robby, what do you remember when you were young? What is the earliest memory you have?"

"Drinking my uncle's beer," he said.

"Do you remember being hugged or rocked?" I asked.

No, he replied. He looked at me sitting in an office chair and asked, "Would you rock me?"

I opened my arms and said, "Come here."

25

I rocked Robby for the rest of the hour with neither of us saying a word. He hugged me around the neck and rested his head on my shoulder. (I knew I could get in a lot of trouble for touching a child, let alone rocking them. But this little boy needed to be held and rocked.)

The following day Robby talked through the entire session. He told me that his friend, who rode bikes with him every day, was killed. He didn't know why or who did it, but he was dead. Nothing in Robby's records showed that his best friend had been murdered, but when it all came out, his friend was the victim of a drive-by shooting. He wasn't allowed to go to the funeral. No one acknowledged his friend's death or talked to him. He stopped riding his bike or talking to anyone. He became depressed and despondent, except to show anger by tearing things up and trying to stab himself.

We continued our play therapy. Robby talked throughout each session. I had a large poster board with colored markers. I drew a picture of him in the middle of it and wrote down his good qualities on the poster around the drawing. I put it on the door of his room and asked all the residents and staff to write or draw something nice about Robby. He came into our session one day saying, "You know what, Ms. Patricia, people like me. People really like me. I didn't even like me. Now I find out that everybody likes me, and even I like me."

He showed me his poster and all the good things people had said about him.

26

Robby had buried his feelings, and when we bury them, we bury them alive. They later come out in the form of rage and self-destruction. When he was able to look at what had actually happened to his friend, he found healing. Robby was mad at his mother, himself and everyone. He thought no one cared.

Gary Hides His Depression with Intellectual Conversations

Gary, 16, a patient in the Psychiatric Ward did not appear suicidal to me. He had an excellent vocabulary and was open, friendly and funny. At 5'10", with brown hair, a good build, and brown eyes, he seemed like any other high functioning, junior in high school. He played on the football team, enjoyed playing the lead in the school play and made straight A's. He enjoyed science, but his favorite subject was psychology. He showed no signs of depression and could talk about Schizophrenia, Bipolar Disorder, and Borderline Personality as well as any counselor. He seemed to be knowledgeable about almost any subject we talked about. He was upbeat, friendly and fun to talk to.

Each week the doctors, social workers, and counselors had a meeting to discuss various patients. Gary hid his depression with enthusiasm, jokes and great conversation. He could speak the language of Social Workers and Psychologists. When Gary's name came up, I discovered he had attempted suicide several times. Being an intelligent young man, Gary covered up his feelings with

27

intellectual conversations.   He hid severe clinical depression by being highly knowledgeable in many areas. He knew a little about a lot of subjects and could talk with intelligence to almost anyone.

He was diagnosed with "Borderline Personality," which caused him to be confused about his identity and suicidal at times.   He hid his emotional pain with words so no one could see him as weak or vulnerable.   He was a perfectionist, feeling he needed to control everything. Once I understood what he was doing, I let him know he didn't have to cover his feelings with me.   He could tell me what he really felt - *FEAR*.   His sense of abandonment and despair poured out the day I let him know I would be leaving in two weeks.   He cried hysterically telling me that everyone abandoned him.   Instead of going away by himself to attempt suicide, he poured his heart out to me. Over the next two weeks, he was able to share feelings he had never told anyone.   Instead of burying them, he poured them out and found healing, love, and acceptance in the midst of his pain.

Most of the youth in the Psychiatric Ward had been diagnosed with Borderline personality disorder.

"Borderline Personality Disorder"

Borderline personality disorder (BPD), causes a confused self-image and feelings of worthlessness. Individuals with this disorder may push others away even though they may desire to have loving and lasting relationships. It affects how they feel about themselves and how they relate to others. Anger, impulsiveness and mood swings can often overwhelm them.

Symptoms of Borderline Personality Disorder

- Destructive behavior such as cutting, suicide attempts, risky driving, gambling, illegal drug use, etc.
- Extreme mood swings.
- Anxiety.
- Depression.
- Anger and antagonistic behavior.
- Impulsiveness.
- Difficulty controlling emotions.
- Feels misunderstood, neglected, alone, empty or hopeless.
- Fear of being alone.
- Feelings of self-hate.
- Fear of being abandoned.

Borderline personality disorder causes an insecure self-image. One's self-identity often changes. An unstable self-image leads to frequent changes in jobs, friendships, goals, and values.

Relationships are usually in turmoil. They may idealize someone one moment, but that feeling can abruptly shift to fury and hate over a minor misunderstanding. People with borderline personality disorder have difficulty accepting gray areas, seeing the world as black or white, good or bad, right or wrong.

When to See a Doctor

If you or someone you love has any of the signs or symptoms above, talk to your doctor or a mental health provider. Treatment can help one feel better and live a stable, rewarding life.

If you notice signs or symptoms in a family member or friend, talk to that person about seeing a doctor or mental health provider.

4

Catastrophic Grief After the Suicide of a Loved One

Rick Warren's Son Commits Suicide

On April 6, 2013, Pastor Rick Warren's youngest son Matthew, age 27, committed suicide. Pastor Warren and his wife Kay have suffered deep grief over the death of their son who had been diagnosed with borderline personality. Pastor Warren wrote, *"The Purpose Driven Life,"* a bestselling book that has influenced multitudes. He is the founder of Saddleback Church in Southern California and has been a role model and teacher in the Christian community for decades.

"Matthew had a brilliant intellect and a gift for sensing who was most in pain or most uncomfortable in a room. He'd then make a bee-line to that person to engage and encourage them," Rick Warren wrote to his church staff after he learned of Matthew's death. "But only those closest knew that he struggled from birth with mental illness, dark holes of depression, and even suicidal thoughts. In spite of America's best doctors, medication, counselors, and prayers for healing, the torture of mental illness never subsided." [1]

Matthew was highly intelligent and sensitive. Some of the smartest, compassionate, caring people in this world have battled depression and suicide. Many Christians want to know, "Is suicide a sin?" Yes, I believe it is a sin of unbelief. "Can a person who commits suicide go to heaven?" YES - Going to heaven does not depend on being perfect. It is what Christ did for us on that Cross, over 2,000 years ago that gives us the ability to go to heaven. *"We are saved by grace through faith and not of ourselves lest any man should boast."* (Eph. 2:8-9)

"I am comforted and grateful that my son, Matthew is now in heaven and his 'broken mind' is finally healed," said Kay Warren. "This is not how it should be. But this is how it is. And I still, at the end of the day, trust in God's goodness."

They kept Matthew's illness from the public for the sake of his dignity. "We didn't want him to endure the scrutiny that's being thrown at Rick. He was already struggling," said Ms. Warren. "To be in the public spotlight, having people scrutinizing him … he didn't need that."

Catastrophic Grief of A Family After A Suicide

[2]Kay Warren describes Catastrophic Grief: she said after Matthew's death her family experienced it. Kay outlined what this kind of grief looks like:

- Anger: Nowhere to place it; the person one loves is the killer.
- Guilt: Almost everybody ends up feeling guilty.

- What If: Should I have done more? What if I had said this? What if I had done this?
- All consuming: Keep replaying the day that the suicide happened over and over again.
- Exhausting: This kind of grief is hard work.
- Along: Lonely, Isolating: It feels like it's just me and the universe and God.
- Life: Life will never be the same again, but life will be good again.
- Other: It opens up other un-grieved, un-mourned, and incomplete losses.

"I have to tell you that I fully expect for the rest of my life, as long as I live, there will be tears in my eyes. And I won't ultimately be comforted until God Himself wipes it from my face," said Kay to an audience of people who have also survived losing a loved one to suicide.

[3]Kay quoted Eric Liddell, Olympic gold medalist runner in the 1924 Munich Games, "Circumstances may appear to wreck our lives and God's plans. But God is not helpless among the ruins. Our broken lives are not lost or useless. God's love is still working. He comes in and takes the calamity and uses it victoriously, working out his wonderful plan of love."

Kay said, "Every morning when I wake up and every night when I put my head on the pillow, the reality occurs again. He's not here, and he's not coming back. But I know that Matthew is OK. He went straight into the arms of Jesus

Christ when his body hit the ground on earth; he was in the presence of God."

A Reason To Live: My beloved friends - If you are in emotional pain thinking suicide is your only answer, imagine what it would do to your family and friends. I realize when you are suffering it is hard to think of other people. But for a moment imagine how your parents, brothers and sisters, children, mate, and friends would feel. Please call someone. Get help! You do not want to leave a legacy of suicide with your family and your loved ones.

5

Suicide at the Battered Women's Shelter

Suicide Begins in the Mind

Suicide starts in our thoughts. When the mind is filled with painful thoughts, death may seem the only way out. At the battered women's shelter, suicide often appeared less painful than life with an abusive mate. Most of the ladies I worked with at the shelter had "Post-Traumatic Stress Disorder" (PTSD), and many were suicidal. PTSD occurs when someone has experienced a traumatic event and had flashbacks and anxiety from the memory of it. One out of four victims of abuse attempts suicide.

Most of the ladies at the shelter were Christians. Ministers and church members often told the abused, battered women, "God hates divorce. You cannot leave your mate. You need to pray for him. You must stay and trust God. Christ uses these trials to make you more like Him."

Linda was married to a violent, abusive man who was a deacon at their church. When she came to the shelter, she was suicidal and depressed but chose life because of her three children. As she began to heal emotionally and physically, she started talking about returning to her abusive husband. I begged her not to go. She left the shelter with her three children saying, "God hates divorce. He would never forgive me if I left him."

I prayed for God to give Linda a way out. She came back to the shelter three weeks later saying, "I discovered my husband did not divorce his previous wife. I am free! I am not legally married to him."

We were able to help Linda get a job, an apartment, furniture, clothes and a good school for the children. She found a new church where she was loved and supported.

Childhood Verbal Abuse Leads to Suicidal Thoughts

In a large room on the main floor of the shelter, I was putting chairs in a circle to conduct a "Life Skills" group. Three ladies arrived early, "Ms. Patricia, we are worried about Carrie. She keeps talking about suicide."

Carrie shuffled into the room with her hair sticking out of big pink rollers. It was two in the afternoon, but she still wore her robe and slippers. Her eyes were puffy, and half closed as she dropped into a chair.

Fourteen girls were all in a circle waiting for me to say something. I looked straight at Carrie and said, "The ladies all tell me you have been talking about committing suicide."

Big tears rolled down Carrie's face. "I'm ugly and stupid," she said. "I would be better off dead."

"Where did that lie come from?" I asked.

The names that went through her mind began as a little girl when her father got drunk and called her names. The names were engraved on her mind and had become a part of her identity. "You're stupid and ugly. Get out of here! I don't want to look at your ugly face," he yelled in an alcoholic rage.

How can I love myself after he said those things about me?"

I took a piece of paper and folded it down the middle. "Let's see Carrie. Your father called you, 'Stupid and ugly.' What else did he call you?"

Carrie gave me a long list of ugly words he used such as, "Bitch, tramp, whore,......."

I wrote each of them down on one side of the paper. "Alright Carrie, you have told me what your father said. Now tell me who you really are. The other ladies think you are a giving person that cares about others. Is that right?"

The group members along with Carrie all joined in to help with the list. "Carrie is smart," they said. "She got her associates degree making straight A's. Carrie cares about us. She would give us the shirt off her back. In fact, she was giving all her stuff away this morning. She is beautiful when she fixes herself up."

"I am a caring person," Carrie said. "I love people; maybe too much. I am a faithful friend. I love animals. I am a kind person."

I wrote each of these attributes down. Then I held up the paper for Carrie and the whole group to look at. "Is it true that the words stupid and ugly on this side of the paper are what your father said when he was drunk? Did he say these things when he was sober?"

"Oh no," said Carrie. "I was his little princess when he was sober."

"It sounds to me like you have let alcohol define who you are," I said. "Did your father call you these cruel names or did the alcohol tell you that? Reality, truth and logic are not in a person who is drunk."

"I never thought of it that way," said Carrie. "When he was sober I was his beautiful, smart little girl."

"Let's look at what you and your friends have said about you," I said, "kind, caring, beautiful, loving and giving."

"Which side of this paper is the truth about Carrie," I asked. "You have believed a lie. And you married another alcoholic who confirms what your father said."

A smile covered Carrie's face. The truth set her free.

Carrie tried to fix her childhood hurts by marrying another alcoholic. When he became physically and verbally abusive, she fled to a battered women's shelter. She gave

38

up hope when she could not get her father or husband to change.

I passed papers out to each of the ladies in the group. "I want each of you to write down the negative things others have said about you on one side of the paper. Then I want you to write the truth on the other part. We are going to reprogram our minds with the truth, identifying the lies we have believed. Each of you has tried to fix your childhood abuses by connecting with those who treat you the same way your abusive caregiver treated you. You cannot fix anyone but yourself. No one has the right to define who you are but God. Rather than getting involved with those who are as rejecting and abusive as your caregivers were, you need to nurture and care for the hurt little girl inside you. She needs you to respect, love, protect and validate her."

Jesus said, *"You will know the truth, and the truth will set you free."* (John 8:32 NIV)

Inner Healing by Nurturing the Child Within

I did assessments on each young lady that came into the shelter using genealogies to get a view of their background. As I looked at their parents and grandparents, a pattern formed. The ladies often picked mates who abused them, in the same way, one of their caregivers did. A daughter of an alcoholic may marry an alcoholic. The daughter of a mentally ill mother or father may marry a mentally ill man. They were unable to see the red lights to prevent them

39

from mating with an abuser. They sought to fix what they could not fix as little girls.

In a group session, I asked the girls to close their eyes and imagine the little girl inside them. I then asked them to imagine a loving, caring adult protecting them. Now I want you to hear the adult saying, "I am your adult. I am here to take care of you."

Now I want you to imagine God has a big chain cutter. He is cutting the chains of abuse from your past and present. You are no longer in bondage to your abusive caregiver or your abusive mate.

This was only the beginning of healing for the *little girls* that came to the shelter as ladies trying to fix their abused childhoods. Jesus came to heal the broken-hearted, set the captive free and open the eyes of the blind. They were in bondage. A stronghold of false beliefs had taken control of their lives affecting many of the decisions they made. God gives us the power to break strongholds through the truth. *"The weapons we fight with are not the weapons of the world. On the contrary, they have divine power to demolish strongholds. We demolish arguments and every pretension that sets itself up against the knowledge of God, and we take captive every thought to make it obedient to Christ."* (2 Cor. 10:4-5. NIV)

Victims Think Suicide is the Only Way Out

Many women feel the only way out is death. Getting out of an abusive or violent relationship isn't easy. The hope that

40

things will change keeps the victim from leaving. There is also the fear of what the partner will do if he/she discovers the victim is trying to leave. The victim feels trapped and helpless. But help is available. There are many resources available for abused and battered women, including crisis hotlines, shelters—even job training, legal services, and childcare. If you are a victim, you deserve to live free of fear. Start by reaching out!

Emergency Room Intervention

I was "on-call" to the emergency room of the local hospital when a woman came in who was battered. My job was to show her the options available to her. There were times when the abuser was actually out in the waiting room, and although the victim wanted to go to a shelter, she was not free to go. In one case where the husband was in the waiting room, the lady I counseled with said, "It was worth getting my arm broke to be able to talk to you. You are the first person I have spoken to other than my husband in three years."

I gave her the number of the battered woman's shelter I worked at and told her to memorize it. My hope was that she would call us. With no phone, no car and no friends she would have a difficult time calling, but I knew from my own experience that she could find a way if she really wanted out.

If you are in a physically or emotionally abusive relationship, God does not want you to be abused. You will NOT be failing God if you leave. Please, do not stay in an abusive relationship. God does not want you to be unequally yoked with an abuser. *"Don't become partners with those who reject God. How can you make a partnership out of right and wrong? That's not a partnership; that's war. Is light best friends with dark? Does Christ go strolling with the Devil? Do trust and mistrust hold hands? Who would think of setting up pagan idols in God's holy Temple? But that is exactly what we are, each of us a temple in whom God lives. God himself put it this way*:

"I'll live in them, move into them; I'll be their God, and they'll be my people. So leave the corruption and compromise; leave it for good," says God. "Don't link up with those who will pollute you. I want you all for myself. I'll be a Father to you; you'll be sons and daughters to me. "The Word of the Master, God. (2 Cor. 6:14-18 MSG)

Why Do Victims Stay?

- They hope the abuser will change. This does not usually happen unless the abuser takes full responsibility for his/her actions. Personally, I have never seen an abuser change. I am not saying it can't happen. I just haven't seen it.
- They believe they can help the abuser. The fact is the victim of abuse cannot change the abuser. Removing themselves from the abuser is the greatest help they can give.
- Often the victim believes the abuser when they promise to change. There is often a honeymoon

stage after the abuse. But this only lasts a short time.

- The belief that God does not want them to leave but expects them to submit to the abusive mate.
- Does not know where to go or how to support themselves. (There are many shelters where a victim of abuse can find help and housing.)
- Fear of losing the children.
- Fear the abuser will hurt them.

The Real Danger of Staying in an Abusive Relationship

It is true that some women get killed when they try to leave an abusive relationship, but more are killed staying in the relationship. Many commit suicide, rather than continuing to be emotionally and/or physically abused.

If you are in an abusive relationship, emotionally and/or physically, I encourage you to protect yourself and your children. Set a standard; let the abuser know how you expect to be treated. If the abuse continues, you may have to leave. Most battered women's shelters keep the address confidential. The shelter I worked in always picked victim up and brought them to our facility. We were very careful not to let people know our location.

I am sorry that you are going through this. In this country, abuse should not be tolerated. Yet many men, women, and children are being abused. And they often have no one to stand up for them.

Action Steps

1. Stop hiding the abuse from others. It is not your fault. Tell your friends and family, counselors and pastors, what is going on.
2. Keep a bag packed, including money so you can leave.
3. Learn the number of your local Battered Women's Shelter by heart and call it.
4. If you end up at the hospital or doctor's office, ask them to call the Battered Women's Shelter for you and to send someone to pick you up.
5. File charges with the police. You may need documentation of the abuse.
6. Get a restraining order! Protect yourself!
7. Know this: God loves you and doesn't want you and your children to be abused.
8. Do NOT let the abuser know where you are.
9. Whether you are a female or male being emotionally abused by your mate, get counseling. Set a standard of how you expect to be treated. Insist your spouse gets help.
10. Call the national domestic abuse hotline: 1-800-799-SAFE (7233), or 1-800-787-3224 (TTY).

6

Childhood Sexual Abuse
"It's Not Your Fault."

Shirley, 54, dealt with severe bouts of depression which left her unable to function for weeks at a time. My experience with Post-Traumatic Stress and Inner Healing motivated her husband, a deacon at my church, to ask me to help his wife. I went to Shirley and asked if she would like to meet me on Saturday and have a confidential counseling session. "Oh, please," she asked. "Would you really do that for me?"

That Saturday we met at our church in a quiet room. We began our counseling session with prayer. "Father, would you remove the dark thoughts in Shirley's mind that cause her depression and despair."

"Do you know why you get so depressed?" I asked Shirley.

"Yes, no one knows how evil I am. Not even my husband," she said as tears filled her eyes.

"Could you tell me what makes you feel this way?" I asked.

"I had a baby when I was 12 years old. She was adopted," she said.

"Who was the father," I asked.

"My own dad was the father," she said. "From the age of nine until I was twelve, he was having sex with me. My mother died when I was nine, and that was when my dad started coming into my room at night. Then he started making me come to his bed, and I had to sleep with him every night. "

Shirley went to the home of some loving foster parents after having the baby. She went on to finish junior high and high school. The foster family loved Shirley and took her to church with them. She met her husband at church and married as soon as she graduated. After going to the maternity home, she never saw her birth father again. No one talked to her about the baby, her father or the guilt she carried.

"I am so bad" she said. "No one knows about my baby girl except my foster parents, and they never talked about it. I am so bad I don't think God can love and forgive someone like me."

"Do you believe it was your fault he had sex with you?"

"Yes," she said. "Who else's fault would it be?"

"The job of your father was to protect you," I said. "You were a little girl. His job was to be your protector, but instead, he became your perpetrator."

The child within Shirley felt grief, shame, and guilt. She was too ashamed to tell anyone what happened. She couldn't love herself so she could not imagine anyone else loving her.

"The most important thing you need to know today is," I said, "**It is NOT your fault**. It was your father's sin, not yours. You don't need to carry it any longer."

Shirley Cares for The Child Within

Shirley processed her childhood sexual abuse the way a child would see it. She took on the guilt and shame a child would feel. She felt it was her fault thinking she could have stopped it. I encouraged Shirley to look at the situation as an adult. She was now an adult, and her job was to protect, nurture and love the little girl inside her, who had been so grossly abused.

"I want you to look at this now as an adult would see it," I told her. "Do you see that little girl that is nine, ten or eleven years old? Tell her it was not her fault! Tell her that you are going to take care of her because her daddy didn't protect her, but *you* will protect her."

Shirley began to talk. "I can see that little girl. I am going to take care of her from now on. God did intervene. He put her in a loving foster home and gave her a loving husband. God loves that little girl. And I will love her too."

Shirley's transformation was amazing as she stopped carrying the guilt and shame of her father's sexual abuse.

Girls In Juvenile Court System

I sat with a group of 30 girls ages 11-17 who were living in a juvenile court facility. I was having a discussion on, "Respecting Authority." A small 13-year-old became enraged when I told them they needed to respect their parents. "I don't have to respect my stepfather," she screamed.

"Does your stepfather put a roof over your head and food on the table?" I asked.

"I can't respect him," she said. "He raped me."

I sat in shock not knowing how to respond.

"I can't respect my mother's boyfriend because he raped me," another young lady shouted.

I put my group papers down along with all my preconceived ideas of what the girls needed. "You tell me what you have been going through," I said. "How many of you have been raped or sexually abused in any way?"

Half of the girls had been sexually abused by a relative, friend of their family or stepfather. I listened as the girls poured out one heartbreaking story after another telling of devastating sexual, mental and physical abuses. A sixteen-year-old told of how she killed her mother's boyfriend.

48

"I was standing in the kitchen," she said. "That man had already raped me four times. I decided I was not going to let him hurt me one more time. When he tried to attack me, I pulled a knife out of the drawer and stabbed him. I didn't mean to kill him. I just wanted to stop him. That is why I am in here."

In the 13 years, I worked at the court at least half the girls from ages seven to seventeen had been sexually abused. Many of those who had not been abused sexually were abused physically and/or emotionally. I heard of every kind of abuse imaginable. Most of them had never been able to tell anyone about their trauma. When many tried to tell someone, they were blamed or told they were lying.

These were children; not hardened criminals. They were girls who were hurt, violated and treated as *things* rather than kids that needed guidance and protection. Many of the girls blamed themselves. I told them, "It was NOT your fault. You were violated by those who were supposed to be protecting you. You are God's precious gift."

Many of them were depressed and suicidal. Being able to talk about the abuse helped these girls to stop blaming themselves.

[4]Sexually Abused Youth May Attempt Suicide

Some of the behaviors a sexually abused youth may exhibit are:

- Suicide attempts

- Unusual interest in or avoidance of all things of a sexual nature
- Fear or dislike of certain places or people
- Sleep disturbances
- School problems
- Withdrawing from family, friends and normal activities
- Poor hygiene
- Return to younger, more babyish behavior
- Depression
- Anxiety
- Discipline problems
- Running away
- Eating disorders
- Passive or overly pleasing behaviors
- Delinquent acts
- Low self-esteem
- Self-destructive behavior
- Hostility or Aggression
- Drug or alcohol problems
- Sexual activity or pregnancy at an early age

Child Sexual Abuse Statistics

[5]The statistics on childhood sexual abuse are incomplete. Much abuse is never reported. Nine studies from ten countries, with a total of almost 9,000 participants, showed that those who experienced Childhood Sexual Abuse, before the age of 16 to 18 were more than twice as likely to attempt or complete suicides. Studies by David Finkelhor[6],

Director of the "Crimes Against Children Research Center," show that:

- One in five girls and one in twenty boys are victims of childhood sexual abuse, (CSA)
- Self-report studies show that 20 percent of adult females and 5-10 percent of adult males recall a childhood sexual assault or sexual abuse incident
- During a one-year period in the U.S., 16 percent of youth ages 14 to 17 had been sexually victimized
- Over the course of their lifetime, 28 percent of U.S. youth ages 14 to 17 had been sexually victimized
- Children are most vulnerable to Childhood Sexual Abuse between the ages of 7 to 13
- According to a 2003 National Institute of Justice report, three out of four adolescents who have been sexually assaulted were victimized by someone they knew well.

How to Help a Victim of Rape or Childhood Abuse

There are two important things you can do when talking with someone who has been the victim of Childhood Sexual Abuse or Rape. **LISTEN!** Let them know *"IT IS NOT THEIR FAULT."* You really can't help anyone if you go into a situation with a pat formula and think using it will help. Often persons who have been sexually violated, blame themselves. If they were attracted to or stimulated in any way by the abuser, they might feel it was their fault. It is hard to tell someone about a sexual violation. So if someone tells you about being sexually violated, the worst thing you can do is blame the victim. Asking questions like, "How were you dressed?" "What did you say or do to cause them to..." "Why did you let them in your house?" "Were you attracted to them in the first place?" Any questions that appear to be accusations will hurt rather than help and cause the victim to close up.

You can be that one safe person to whom that victim can talk. You can let them know that it was not their fault.

If someone trusts you enough to tell you of childhood sexual abuse, look at it as a gift from God, they shared with you. Let them know that it was not their fault. Listen! Care! Encourage!

If you have been the victim of sexual abuse, the one thing you need to know is, "It is NOT your fault!" Even if you were flattered by the perpetrator, it is still not your fault. Predators use flattery to seduce. *It is not your fault*.

7

New Life After the Death of a Loved One

Severe Grief

Losing a loved one can put us into a state of grief so severe that it seems it will last forever. Some isolate and cannot find the energy to interact with others. Some think of suicide as the only way out of the pain. I met my husband Richard while conducting a Grief and Loss class. His story shows a healthy way to deal with the grief of losing a loved one. He stayed active and participated in Grief and Loss classes at a nearby hospital and a local church. He found a support group. He forced himself to eat healthy although he didn't feel like eating. He made himself get up and go to church even though he felt numb inside. He decided to do whatever he had to do to get through the grief, rather than "stuffing" it.

There is a process for getting through the grieving. See how Richard Dascher walked through the process, although it was very painful at times.

Journey through the Death of My Wife

By Dr. Richard Dascher

I lay in bed unable to sleep. Thoughts tumbled around in my head like a kaleidoscope of crazy colors. I could not focus or concentrate on anything. I could not face the reality of what had happened that day. No, I was not doing drugs. My wife, June had just died, and I never felt like this before in my entire life. I couldn't think. Everything kept spinning around in a blur of crazy colors. I was in the first stage of grief - "SHOCK."

My whole life changed – nothing would ever be the same again. My hopes and dreams for the future had come to an end. A few hours before, I was driving in the car to a Christmas party at church with my wife. We were chatting about the day's activities, and the weekend we had just spent together in San Antonio on the River Walk. It had been a celebration of lighting the Christmas lights along the river. We had a great time together.

We arrived at Church, sat at a table with other deacons and their wives playing games. We laughed and had a great time with our friends. We got up to leave. I took hold of June's hand. We stopped to hug and talk to a few friends on the way out. Then all of a sudden June made a funny sound and slumped to the ground. A deacon and his wife, both MD's, started to do CPR immediately. I vaguely remember the people getting into a circle and praying. After that, everything became a blur.

We had been married 38 years and were preparing for retirement with an exciting cruise planned to celebrate the occasion. That had been our dream for some time. We bought land in a beautiful area where we would build our retirement home. How could all of this be gone so suddenly? No warnings; No "goodbyes": nothing but stark, empty, loneliness. How was I to live without my life long partner? All my hopes, dreams, and future, were centered around June.

I went back to work that January. My mom, our children, and friends had all gone back to their normal lives. My first grandson, Nicholas was born prematurely a few months after her death. This accentuated my grief knowing June had looked forward to seeing her first grandchild.

I was extremely fortunate to have friends like Richard and Ann Norton, who supported me through the long months of the grieving process, by inviting me out and talking to me. They helped keep me involved in life when it would have been easy to give up. Richard's Christmas gift to me was a day planner with dates of activities they had planned for us to do together, already penciled in. They were God's gift to me in my time of greatest need. Friends often abandon a widow or widower because they don't know what to say and feel uncomfortable around them. Some told me they didn't call for fear of saying or doing the wrong thing and making my grief worse. But it is in times of mourning that caring friends who listen much and speak little are needed. When everyone goes home is when the hard work of grieving begins.

A Definition of Grief Work Is Summarized by the Acronym "TEAR"

T = To accept the reality of the loss
E = Experience the pain of the loss
A = Adjust to the new environment without the lost object
R = Reinvest in the new reality

I continued to go to Church each Sunday although I did not feel like it. I felt little, except sadness and loneliness. I knew that this was part of the grief path, and I needed help if I was to make it out of the wilderness of sorrow. I started looking and praying for sources that could help me. I was able to find a grief support group at a local hospital. This was a significant beginning in getting through the grief journey.

The real break-through came when I saw a note in our church bulletin that announced a nine-week Grief and Loss class taught by a Social Worker at another church. I did not know what to expect and went with some fear and doubt. That all seemed to be put away when we were greeted by a beautiful, smiling lady named Patricia, who was to be the leader of this group.

After just a few weeks of class, I came to realize that I had two choices. I could be like the "Children of Israel" and wonder in circles in the desert for forty years. Or I could go to the "Promised Land," confront the giants and get on with my life. It wasn't easy, but I was certain I did not want to be in the desert of despair any longer than necessary. I could have chosen depression, isolation or even suicide. But I made the choice of doing the hard work of dealing openly and honestly with my grief.

Our teacher walked with us through the grief process showing us how to express our feelings, so we did not bury them. "When you bury a "feeling," you bury it alive, and it will keep coming back up in one way or another," she said. "It's OK to cry and feel the pain of this loss."

She taught us that there are actually more than "Five Stages of Grief" but experts have narrowed them down to make them easy for the layperson to remember. No two people are alike; therefore, no one grieves the same way or at the same pace. The key is to be able to get through the stages to a place of acceptance so we can live again.

Stages of Grief.

1. *Denial*

2. *Anger*

3. *Bargaining*

4. *Depression*

5. *Acceptance*

Writing A Goodbye Letter

One of the hardest things I had to do was write a "goodbye" letter to June. Patricia encouraged me to take the time I needed to write the letter but stressed that it was an important part of my healing.

Saying "Goodbye" in that letter was one of the most emotionally challenging things I have ever done. It took me about three weeks to get up the courage to do it, but I felt a great sense of freedom when it was completed.

In the classes, I learned how to define who I am. I discovered my identity was not "June's husband," nor was I just a father or a Chemical Engineer. Our roles in life can change, but my real identity, my true identity is God's Child, and that will never change or be taken from me.

A Future and a Hope

One day near the end of the nine-week class time my instructor said, "Before you leave, God has given me a scripture to share with you."

She opened her Bible to Jeremiah 29: 11-13. *"For I know the plans for you,' says the Lord, 'plans for good and not for evil; to give you a future and a hope. In those days when you pray, I will listen, and when you seek me you will find me when you look for me in earnest"*.

God had shown me that scripture before, but on that day, it was like living water to my empty soul. It filled me with new hope knowing that God had a future for me. The road out of grief was the most emotionally painful road I have ever traveled. I can't imagine anything more devastating than losing a mate. The nights were long and lonely. I

58

wanted to run away, stuff it, hide it and forget but God continued to encourage me to walk through the desert of grief to a new land and stage of life filled with new hopes and joys.

I stayed in touch with my teacher through e-mail. A couple years after the classes had ended I sent Patricia a note asking if she would like to meet me at Cracker Barrel to go over my progress.

Patricia sat across the table from me listening to me talk about everything from how I learned to be a caring husband, to my recent trip to the Virgin Islands. We both laughed and talked until the waitress asked us to leave saying, "The lunch crowd is coming in now. Would you let us use this table?"

I could not remember ever enjoying a conversation more than I did that morning. Patricia's loving smile and beautiful green eyes radiated life like no one I had ever known before. I felt an overflowing joy being able to share so openly with another Christian, who accepted me unconditionally. I told her my story again and shared things that I had done and learned through all my years of marriage. When the waitress asked us to leave, I walked her out to her car and asked if she would like to go to dinner. That evening I picked her up at her apartment, and we decided on seafood. Again we talked for hours enjoying every moment we had together. When I took her home, I began thinking immediately of where I could take her on our next date and the fun activities we could experience together.

Patricia and I were married on July 7, 2001. My friend Richard Norton was my best man. Patricia and I developed our life mission, *"To heal the brokenhearted and set the captive free."* Our mission sent us to Uganda where we adopted several children and young men. We put several young men through Seminary. We opened our home on Sunday nights to have Shepard Groups where we talked, prayed and studied the Bible. Together we retired to the scenic Lake of the Ozarks in Missouri. We began publishing Soul Magazine and distributed it throughout the area. Patricia took a position as Executive Director of the local Pregnancy Help Center, and I became their Business Manager. We celebrated our wedding anniversary last summer on a Riverboat in Branson, Mo. We have traveled all over the world: Alaska, Uganda, St. Croix, Seoul, Korea, and Cambodia.

We still talk and laugh together for hours at a time. We enjoy reading our Bibles together and know God is the most important part of our lives. Together we continue to have a new "Future and Hope."

Grief Takes Time

Living through the loss of a mate takes time and courage. Everyone grieves differently. Richard knew he had to stay active. Working through this pain by going to grief and loss classes was not easy, but necessary to go on to live a full and joyous life. We know life will be different. Not necessarily bad, just different. Richard's friends would not let him completely isolate himself by giving him a planner and penciling in dates and times they would do things together. Some time alone is good, but too much isolation can lead to depression which sometimes turns to Clinical Depression and suicidal thoughts.

Take Care of Yourself

This is the time to take care of you. Get involved with activities and people you enjoy. Watch joyful movies, read uplifting books, get around people who love you.

God Loves Us Even When We Don't Understand

When my sister in law Tammy died at the age of 47, her daughter asked me, "Why would God take my mother?" "I don't know why God does some things," I told her. "I know He loves us, and I trust Him even when I don't understand."

God miraculously heals some people, and He brings others home where they are totally and permanently healed. That is my greatest comfort when someone I love dies.

I believe everyone who goes through the crisis of the death of a loved one needs to get support. But if the following symptoms occur it is imperative to seek help immediately.

- Suicidal thoughts
- Guilt

- Anxiety
- Depression
- Panic attacks
- Difficulty sleeping
- Extreme weight gains or losses

Healthy Ways to Deal With Grief and Loss

1. Get up and get dressed in the morning.

2. Eat a healthy breakfast.

3. Find a support group to be involved with.

4. Look into churches, organizations, and hospitals that provide "Grief and Loss Classes."

5. Do something special for yourself. Get a movie you would enjoy or something you have been wanting. Call someone you would enjoy talking to.

6. Keep a journal of your thoughts. When you bury a feeling, you bury it alive. Write down those feelings.

7. Talk to God. He loves and cares for you. Ask God for anything you want. He might say, "Yes" "No" or "Wait," but He will answer you.

8

Bipolar Disorder (Manic Depression)

What is Bipolar Disorder?

Everyone has their highs and lows in life. Bipolar Disorder (also known as manic depression), is marked by extreme changes in mood, thought, energy and behavior. It is not a character flaw or a sign of personal weakness. Symptoms are extreme changes in moods with mania (highs) and depression (lows). The periods of depression or mania can last for hours, days, weeks or months.

David Mann Asks for Intervention for His Bipolar Son, David, Twenty-Four

David Mann was one of my art teachers and a good friend. He asked if I knew anything about Bipolar Disorder and could help his son. Previously I had worked closely with those who had Bipolar Disorder. Those I had helped had a pattern of quitting their medication thinking they were OK and didn't need it. Some enjoyed getting on a manic high. "My wife and I don't know what to do," Mann said. "We can't get him to go to the hospital or take his medications. I gave him a nice two-bedroom trailer to live in so he could be on his own. We told him all he had to do was pay the utilities. He did fine at his job delivering pizza until he

63

quit taking his medicine. Now he is totally out of control and talking about committing suicide."

How We Helped David Get Medical Assistance

Mann's son was named David, after his father. My husband Richard and I went to see David. He was talking so fast he was hard to understand. The trailer his father gave him was trashed with clothing, dishes and standing water in the bathtub and sink. "I got to get out of this," he said walking back and forth. "The only way out is suicide."

"David, we need to take you to the hospital," I said. "You have gone over the edge. I know the high was euphoric for a time, but you have gone over the edge. You will not survive if we don't get you to the hospital."

David had difficulty hearing me because his mind was racing so fast it kept him from comprehending what I was saying. So I said the same thing in a firm, calm voice over and over again. "David, we need to take you to the hospital. You have gone over the edge. I know you like the high, but you have gone over the edge and must go to the hospital to get your body chemistry back in order."

"Richard and I will take you to the hospital," I said.

"I need to go to the hospital, Patricia. I need to go to the hospital. Will you take me and stay with me? I am getting scared. I have gone over the edge. I've gone over the edge," said David.

In a firm, gentle voice I continued to show David what he needed to do. "Let's get in the car. We are going to the hospital. You need to check yourself in, and I will stay with you. David began repeating what I said."

"I need to go to the hospital. I've gone over the edge. Get in the car. I've gone over the edge. Get in the car."

David got in the back seat of the car. Richard drove as I sat with David seeking to comfort him. "We are going to the hospital," I said. "I will stay with you. "

When we got to the hospital, he signed himself in saying, "I've gone over the edge. I need to be in the hospital. I've gone over the edge."

This was a case in which hospitalization was absolutely necessary. David could not be left by himself. He had to be hospitalized to get stabilized on his medications. I called his father and mother. Terry, his mother, came up to stay with him. "You saved my son's life," she said crying. "Thank you. We didn't know what to do. We couldn't get him to come here to the hospital. We were so scared he would hurt himself, but we didn't know who to call or what to do. We couldn't call the police. They shot a young man last year when his mother called them to help."

The nurses gave David a shot that calmed him down a little. He kept telling his mother over and over again, "Mom, I was going over the edge, so I had to come to the hospital."

Once David was stabilized he talked as he should. David was highly creative and intelligent. But when he didn't take his medications he would either go into a manic state or depression that was so severe he could hardly get out of bed. Both the manic state and the depression could cause him to commit suicide.

David stayed with his parents for a while after he got out of the hospital. He is now living in the trailer and working full time. David will have to be on medication the rest of his life. But he can live a regular, productive, contented life as long as he stays on his medication. His father and mother are both Christians who are active in the homeless ministry where they live, as well as in their church. They have kept David busy with both of these ministries.

Joan 45, Keeps Throwing Away Her Bipolar Disorder Medications

Years ago I helped a lady I'll call Joan. She and her 15-year-old daughter needed a place to stay, so we took her in. Joan went into a manic state, and I didn't know what to do. I had a daycare in my home and two small daughters. Joan began talking a mile a minute. I took her to the hospital where she signed herself in. Over several years, I helped Joan and her teenage daughter. I helped her get stabilized; get a job and a place to live. This had to be done several times since Joan kept going off her medicine and would have to be hospitalized. In one situation, I helped her get a job as a live-in Nanny. As long as she was on her medication, she was all right. But several months later, I got a call from the police. "We are here with Joan, and she is talking about suicide and has a knife. We heard that you have worked with her. We would appreciate it if you would help us get her to the hospital."

I went to the house and drove Joan to the hospital as the police followed. On the way to the hospital, I had her say the Lord's Prayer over and over again.

The hospital helped her get stabilized, but she would need a place to stay. I realized after numerous attempts to help her get a job and a place to live that she needed to be on disability. According to the World Health Organization; Bipolar Disorder is the sixth leading cause of disability in the world.

It can cause severe disability because frequently those who have it quit taking their medicine. Most people don't know how to deal with someone who has gone off their medications. Bipolar Disorder is a treatable illness.

Symptoms of Mania: The "Highs" of Bipolar Disorder

- Heightened mood, exaggerated optimism and self-confidence
- Excessive irritability
- Aggressive behavior
- Inability to sleep
- Grandiose thoughts and inflated sense of self-importance
- Racing speech and thoughts

- Impulsiveness; poor judgment
- Easily distracted
- Uncontrolled behavior such as driving recklessly, jumping off high buildings, talking and acting crazy
- In the most severe cases, delusions and hallucinations
- Suicide attempts

Symptoms of Depression: The "Lows" of Bipolar Disorder

- Prolonged sadness
- Unexplained crying spells
- Sleeps all the time and refuses to get out of bed
- Changes in appetite
- Irritability, anger, worry, agitation, anxiety
- Pessimism, indifference
- Loss of energy, lethargy
- Feelings of guilt, worthlessness
- Inability to concentrate,
- Indecisiveness
- Social withdrawal
- Unexplained aches and pains
- Recurring thoughts of death or suicide

Who is Affected by Bipolar Disorder?

- [7]There are 5.7 million adult Americans that have Bipolar Disorder.

- [8]The average age of Bipolar Disorder is 25 years when diagnosed, but the illness can start in early childhood or as late as the 40's and 50's.
- The disorder is found in all ages, races, ethnic groups and social classes.
- Bipolar Disorder affects both men and women at the same rate.
- Bipolar Disorder can be inherited; two-thirds of people with Bipolar Disorder have at least one close relative with the illness.
- [9]Bipolar Disorder is the sixth leading cause of disability in the world.
- [10]Children and Adolescents: Bipolar disorder is more likely to affect the children of parents who have the disorder. When one parent has Bipolar disorder, the risk to each child is 15 to 30 percent. When both parents have bipolar disorder, the risk increases to 50 to 75 percent.

About one percent of adolescents ages 14 to 18 showed symptoms of bipolar disorder.

[11]Twenty percent of adolescents with major depression develop bipolar disorder within five years of the onset of depression. [12]Up to one-third of the 3.4 million children and young people with depression in the United States may actually be experiencing the early onset of Bipolar Disorder

When manic, kids and teens, in contrast to adults, are more likely to be irritable and prone to destructive outbursts than to be elated or euphoric. [13]When depressed, there may be many physical complaints such as headaches, and stomach aches, tiredness, poor performance in school, irritability, social isolation, and extreme sensitivity to rejection or failure. Success rates of 70 to 85 percent were once expected with lithium for the acute phase treatment of mania. However, lithium response rates of only 40 to 50 percent are now commonplace.

[14]Women are far more likely to be misdiagnosed with depression and men are misdiagnosed with schizophrenia.

In my experience working with Bipolar, I noticed there is a pattern of throwing their medication away. The manic state creates a high they enjoy. Some think when they feel better, they don't need their meds. After the medication is out of their body, they can go into a severe manic state which can lead to suicide.

I also find it difficult to diagnose a child or a teenager with Bipolar Disorder. Teens already have highs and lows because of hormonal changes. In working at the psychiatric center, we did not diagnose a youth or child with disorders like schizophrenia or bipolar because the variations in a youth's body often mimic bipolar disorder.

If You Think You May Have Bi-Polar

1. Keep a journal of your symptoms.
2. Go to a Psychiatrist who can subscribe medications that can balance your symptoms.
3. Don't go off your medications.

4. If you feel your medications are not right, contact your doctor to adjust them.
5. If your medications make you feel suicidal, tell someone and contact your doctor immediately.
6. If you cannot get a hold of your doctor and you are suicidal, go to your local emergency room or call 911.
7. Get rid of all weapons such as guns.
8. Tell a family member your feelings.
9. Call the suicide hotline:**1-800-273-TALK**

Reason To Live: You have a reason to live. Bipolar can be treated just as any other diseases can be treated. You can live a happy life without the symptoms of bipolar by getting treatment and staying on your medications.

9

Helping the Disabled

Stephanie Disabled Seeks Suicide

Stephani 19, was paralyzed from the neck down, except for the use of one arm and hand when she entered the psychiatric center. She was placed in the psychiatric ward of the hospital after several suicide attempts. A car accident the previous year had left her in a wheelchair. Abandoned by her friends, she was lonely and isolated. Her family did not know what to do with a handicapped daughter. All her hopes and dreams for the future were gone. Without a vision, she did not want to live.

All the youth, ages 12-19, in the psychiatric ward, had attempted suicide. I conducted group sessions several times a week and individual counseling sessions with a few of them. I met with Stephanie two to three times a week. She was filled with anger. After groups, she would ask over and over again, "Why would any of these kids want to commit suicide? They aren't in a wheelchair."

I felt if I could show Stephanie what abilities she had left, I could change her perception of life and herself. "Let's look at what you can do," I told Stephanie.

"Can't do anything," she said. "I have nothing left. I have no reason to live."

"OK, let's look at it this way; you have a sharp mind. You can think and reason. You can read and learn. You have the use of one arm and hand. You can talk."

"What am I supposed to do with that? I am totally dependent on someone to take care of me," she said.

"I have decided to make you my assistant in groups," I told her. "You are going to begin by studying a book on self-esteem, "Feeling Good" by David Burns.[15]

"We are going on an exciting adventure," I told Stephanie on our first visit. "We are going to discover what you have left, rather than what you have lost."

In the following months, we read the book. Each day we discussed Stephanie's good qualities. She was intelligent and often humorous. I taught her to use the typewriter and how to put together handouts from the book she had read. By the time she left the hospital, she and I had conducted several groups on how to see the good in ourselves, others and the world around us. She was a changed person. By looking at what she could do, rather than what she had lost, she found a reason to live.

Joni Becomes a Quadriplegic

[16] Joni Erickson was 17 and had just graduated from high school. She was an athletic teenager who found joy in horseback riding, hiking, tennis, and swimming. She, her sister, Kathy, and their friends went swimming in the Chesapeake Bay on a hot summer day on July 30, 1967.

Joni stood on a dock and dove into the water not realizing it was shallow. She describes her accident in her book *Joni*.

"In a jumble of actions and feelings, many things happened simultaneously. I felt my head strike something hard and unyielding. At the same time, clumsily and crazily, my body sprawled out of control. I felt a loud electric buzzing, a strange sensation. It was something like an electrical shock combined with a vibration. I felt no pain. I heard the underwater sound of crunching, grinding sand. I was lying face down on the bottom. Where? How did I get here? Why are my arms tied to my chest? My thoughts screamed. Hey! I'm caught! I felt the pressure of holding my breath begin to build. I have to breathe soon. Fragments of faces, thoughts, and memories spun crazily around my subconsciousness. My friends. My parents. Things I was ashamed of. Maybe God was calling me to come and explain these actions. Joni! A somber voice echoed down some eerie corridor almost as a summons I'm going to die! I don't want to die! 'Help me, please.'

"Joni!" Kathy called.

" I'm here, I've got to breathe!"

"Joni!"

74

The voice muffled through the water sounded far-off now it was closer! "Joni! Are you all right?

Kathy! My sister sees me. 'Help me, Kathy! I'm stuck.'

"Joni! Are you looking for shells?"

"No! I'm caught down here, grab me! I can't hold my breath any longer.

"Did you dive in here? It's so shallow," I heard Kathy clearly now.

Her shadow indicated she was now above me. I struggled inwardly against panic, but I knew I had no more air. Everything was going dark.

I felt Kathy's arms around my shoulders, lifting.

Oh please, dear God. Don't let me die!

Kathy struggled, stumbled, and then lifted again. Oh God, how much longer? Everything was black, and I felt I was falling while being lifted. Just before fainting, my head broke the water's surface. Air! Beautiful, life-giving, salt-tinged air. I choked in oxygen so quickly, I almost gagged. Gasping, I gulped in mouthfuls.

In the confusion, Kathy took charge. She called a new "Hey, are you okay?" Kathy asked. I blinked to clear my mind and dissolve the confusion it didn't seem to work because I saw my arm was slung lifelessly over Kathy's shoulder, yet I felt it was still tied to my chest.

A nearby swimmer on an inflated raft came over. Together they wrestled me onto it and pushed it toward shore. I heard the raft beneath me slide against the sandy beach.

I tried to get up but felt pinned against the raft. People began to hurry over to see what happened.

"Kathy, I can't move!" I was frightened. I could tell they were too.

"Hold me!"

"I am, Joni!" She lifted my hands to show she was grasping them firmly.

"I can't feel it."

Joni was taken by ambulance to a hospital emergency room. She told the ambulance attendant, "I hate to put you to all this trouble. I think once I catch my breath I'll be okay. I'm sure the numbness will wear off shortly."

At the emergency room, she begged the nurse to tell her what was happening to her. The nurse shrugged and began taking off her rings, saying, "The doctor will be here soon. Now, I'm going to put your jewelry in this envelope. Regulations."

"How long do I have to stay here? Can I go home tonight?"

"I'm sorry. You'll have to ask the doctor. Regulations."

Another nurse came in, opened a drawer and pulled out some shears and began cutting Joni's swim suit off. "Don't cut it," Joni begged. "It's brand new."

A doctor came in with a long pin asking if Joni could feel various parts of her body. Joni had no feeling until he reached the top of her shoulders. They took out some electric hair clippers and began shaving Joni's head. "Please," Joni cried. "Not my hair."

Joni suffered a fracture between the fourth and fifth cervical levels and became a quadriplegic, paralyzed from the shoulders down. While undergoing rehabilitation she experienced, anger, depression, and suicidal thoughts. Joni came up with a plan of how to commit suicide. Because she had lost the use of her hands, she tried to talk her friend into killing her. Her friend refused.

Joni learned to paint with a brush between her teeth while in rehabilitation. She continued to paint after she got home. Her father coordinated a showing of her artwork. Today one can buy everything from greeting cards to prints of her work. Since the accident, she's written over forty books, recorded several musical albums, starred in an autobiographical movie of her life called, *Joni*, and developed an organization called, *Joni and Friends*. She has a daily five-minute radio program, heard on over 1,000 broadcast outlets. They sponsor family retreats called the "Wounded Warrior Getaway." "Wheels for the World" collects wheelchairs, which are refurbished by prison inmates and donated to people in developing nations where physical therapists fit each chair to a needy disabled child or adult.

Joni married Ken Tada in 1982. They live in Calabasas, California. In 2010, she announced that she had been diagnosed with breast cancer. She emerged successfully from cancer surgery and is hopeful of a good prognosis. I have read many of Joni's books and seen the movie, *Joni*, several times. God has taken the broken pieces of her life and put her together to help multitudes of people with disabilities and those like myself who need to know that no matter what happens God is in control.

We are all "differently-abled." I can't paint pictures with a brush between my teeth or sing. Joni can do both quite well. God has helped her to use every ability she has to the fullest. The key to dealing with a disability is to look at what skills are left and to use them fully. Joni Eareckson-Tada has helped millions of people throughout her life. In her recent battle with breast cancer, she continued to look at the ways God could use this trial for good. As Joni trusted God and used her talents for good, she found a reason to live.

Overcoming A Disability

We all have disabilities, but we all have abilities as well. I can't start a lawnmower, chop wood or do many of the physical things my husband can do. But I can lay out a newsletter, counsel a troubled youth, speak in front of an audience and write. I can clean a kitchen and cook a good meal. There are many activities I can do. We need to look at what we can do and exult our gifts. I could try all day to start that gas mower, and it would do nothing but frustrate me. But if I spend the day cooking, cleaning, writing, reading or walking I can do those things well.

When you discover, you have a disability look at what you **can do**. What could Stephanie still do even though she could no longer walk? What could Joni still do? Joni had no idea she could paint with a brush between her teeth. What can YOU do? Suicide is not an answer. Multitudes have suffered disabilities and lived up to and beyond their potential. Look at what you have and use it. We are only responsible for what we have. Those who are faithful with little will be given much.

Look Beyond Handicap to Abilities

As he walks on stage slowly, some in the audience hold their breath, praying he does not fall. He sits in a chair and puts his crutches down as he picks up his violin. Itzhak Perlman was a victim of polio when he was four, but few people look at that anymore. All they see is the greatest violin player in the world.

When he was a boy, people had trouble looking beyond his handicap to see the great gift of music he wanted to share with the world. As he continued to play the violin for audiences, they no longer spoke of his polio, for their ears were filled with the music of his violin. Perlman lives a life beyond the handicap of Polio. "The important thing is what you have to offer," he said.

We Are All Differently Abled

We are all differently abled. I can't sing, fix cars, run a marathon or build a house. There are many areas I am disabled in. I bought a keyboard a few years ago that promised anyone could learn to play it. I tried, but my best efforts failed. I finally asked my nephew Zac to help me learn to play it. After a few hours of working with Zac, I asked, "Do you think I can learn to play?"

"Patty, I think if you worked really hard every day for the rest of your life, eventually you might be able to play a keyboard," he said.

Zac was trying to tell me, in the nicest way he knew how that he did not think I could learn to play the instrument. He can play most any instrument without taking lessons. He has autism but has a supernatural gift for music. As a freshman, he won the talent show at his high school for his ability to sing and dance like Michael Jackson. But if he worked really hard the rest of his life, he would not be able to overcome his autism.

If Zac focuses only on his autism, he could become discouraged. But if he focuses on his abilities and what he can do, he excels.

I don't plan on working the rest of my life to learn the keyboard. I will spend my life looking at what I can do and seek to do it well.

Several years ago I worked for an organization that assisted those who had disabilities to get into their own apartments rather than staying in institutions. We helped them function at the highest level possible. The owner said, "I don't like to call people disabled. I like to call them 'differently-abled' "

It 's hard to become suddenly disabled in some area of life. But if we can focus on what we can still do, rather than what can't we will find hope. And even if we lose all our abilities except our mind, we can still pray. There is no power in heaven or earth greater than the power of prayer.

Things to do When Disabled

1. Look at what you have left and use the abilities you still have.
2. Use all the resources available.
3. If you have hearing problems, consider what is available to help you communicate.
4. If you are visually impaired, seek the help available to assist you.
5. Do an assessment of what you can do.

6. Capacity to be an artist was still within Joni whether she used a brush with her hands or between her teeth. She was still an artist.

By looking at your abilities rather than your disabilities, you will find a reason to live.

10

SAD: Seasonal Affective Disorder

Help! I Need Light

Turn on the lights, open the blinds! Winter is coming with its short sunless days and clouds of depression. Many of us get depressed during the long, cloudy winter months. This is called, "Seasonal Affective Disorder" (SAD). Severe depression can occur with SAD, which could lead to suicide. We can take steps to help prevent depression during dark winter months. The key to overcoming SAD is to get more light. As I sit writing this, I am surrounded by lights in my office to prevent depression on the cloudy days. It is surrounded on three sides by windows. Many who have SAD use tanning beds, but these can be dangerous. These can cause skin damage that leads to cancer. There are safer options such full spectrum lights that detour the onset of SAD.

Women are three times more likely to suffer from it than men. During winter months, it seems my creativity goes away with the sun. My body feels heavy, and I want to sleep a lot. I tend to gain weight and feel depressed. Sunlight produces the hormone serotonin that regulates our appetite and mood. In the winter, we obviously get less sunlight which means less serotonin. Research shows that low serotonin levels can lead to depression. From my own observations, SAD appears to run in families. My mother, brother, sister and daughter all have it.

Seasonal affective disorder is a subtype of major depression that comes and goes based on seasons. Tiredness, low mood and a lack of passion for life are three of the most common symptoms; making the illness a form of depression. While 20 percent of the population suffers from the "winter blues" on some level, two percent suffer to such an extent that it disrupts everyday life and is classified as severe depression.

Fall and Winter SAD

Symptoms can start as early as fall, and in the worst cases, they can go on until late spring. Symptoms of winter depression may include:

- Thoughts of death or suicide
- Irritability
- Feelings of hopelessness and/or pessimism
- Loss of interest or pleasure in activities you normally enjoy
- Difficulty concentrating, remembering details and making decisions
- Tiredness or having no energy
- Dark circles under eyes
- Hypersensitivity to rejection
- Heavy, "leaden" feeling in the arms or legs
- Oversleeping
- Appetite changes, especially a craving for foods high in carbohydrates

- Weight gain
- Sad, anxious or "empty" feelings

SAD may be effectively treated with light therapy, but nearly half the people with SAD do not respond to it alone. Antidepressant medicines and talk therapy can reduce SAD symptoms, either alone or combined with light therapy. Daily doses of vitamin D also may help this condition.

When to See a Doctor

It's not unusual to have some days when you feel down. But if you feel down for days at a time, and you can't get motivated to do activities you normally enjoy, see your doctor. This is especially important if your sleep patterns and appetite have changed or if you feel hopeless, think about suicide, or turn to alcohol or drugs for comfort or relaxation.

Causes of SAD

The specific cause of seasonal affective disorder remains unknown. Some factors that may come into play include:

- Your biological clock (circadian rhythm) - The reduced level of sunlight in fall and winter may cause the onset of SAD. This decrease in sunlight may disrupt your body's internal clock and lead to feelings of depression.
- Serotonin levels - A drop in serotonin, a brain chemical (neurotransmitter) that affects mood, might play a role in SAD. Reduced sunlight can

cause a drop in serotonin that may trigger depression.

- Melatonin levels - The change in season can disrupt the balance of the body's level of melatonin, which plays a role in sleep patterns and mood.

Complications

Take signs and symptoms of SAD seriously. As with other types of depression, SAD can get worse and lead to problems if it's not treated. These can include:

- Suicidal thoughts or behavior
- Social withdrawal
- School or work problems
- Thoughts of death or suicide
- Hearing voices or seeing visions

Treatment can help prevent complications, especially if SAD is diagnosed and treated before symptoms get bad.

Light Therapy

In light therapy, also called phototherapy, you sit a few feet from a light box that exposes you to bright light. A full spectrum light is highly recommended. Light therapy mimics natural outdoor light and appears to cause a change in brain chemicals linked to mood.

Light therapy is one of the first-line treatments for fall-onset SAD. It generally starts working in a few days to two weeks and causes few side effects. Research on light therapy is limited, but it appears to be effective for most people in relieving SAD symptoms.

Before you purchase a light therapy box, talk with your doctor about the best one for you. Familiarize yourself with the variety of features and options so that you buy a high-quality product that's safe and works well for you.

Medications

Some people with SAD benefit from antidepressant treatment, especially if symptoms are severe.

An extended-release version of the antidepressant bupropion (Wellbutrin XL or Aplenzin) may help prevent depressive episodes in people with a history of SAD. Other antidepressants are also commonly be used to treat SAD.

Your doctor may recommend starting treatment with an antidepressant before your symptoms typically begin each year. He or she may also recommend that you continue to take the antidepressant beyond the time your symptoms would usually go away. Keep in mind that it may take several weeks to notice full benefits from an antidepressant. Also, you may have to try different medications before you find one that works well for you and has the fewest side effects.

Lifestyle and Home Remedies

In addition to your treatment plan for seasonal affective disorder, try the following: Make your environment sunnier and brighter.

- Open blinds
- Put lots of lights around where you work in the kitchen, office, etc.
- Trim tree branches that block sunlight
- Add skylights to your home
- Sit closer to bright windows while at home or in the office.
- Get outside
- Take a long walk
- Exercise
- Use a daily vitamin D supplement

Alternative Medicines

Sometimes supplements can help: Herbs and supplements are used to try to relieve depression symptoms though it's not clear how effective these treatments are for seasonal affective disorder. Keep in mind, alternative treatments alone may not be enough to relieve your symptoms. Some alternative treatments may not be safe if you have other health conditions or take certain medications. Talk to your doctor about the herbs and supplements you are taking and how they may react to other medications you are using.

Supplements

- St. John's Wort: This herb is not approved by the Food and Drug Administration (FDA) to treat depression in the United States, but it's a popular depression treatment in Europe. It may be helpful if you have mild or moderate depression, but St. John's Wort should be used with caution. It can interfere with some medications, including antidepressants, HIV/AIDS medications, drugs to prevent organ rejection after an organ transplant, birth control pills, blood-thinning medications and chemotherapy drugs.

- SAMe: Pronounced "SAM-e." This dietary supplement is a synthetic form of a chemical that occurs naturally in the body. The name is short for S-adenosyl–L-methionine (es-uh-den-o-sul-el-muh-THIE-o-neen). Like St. John's Wort, SAMe isn't approved by the FDA to treat depression in the United States, but it's used in Europe as a prescription drug to treat depression. SAMe may be helpful, but more research is needed. SAMe may trigger mania in people with Bipolar Disorder.

- Melatonin: This dietary supplement is a synthetic form of a hormone occurring naturally in the body that helps regulate mood. A change in the season to less light may decrease the level of melatonin in your body. Taking melatonin could reduce winter-onset SAD, but more research is needed. Have you ever noticed how children and teenagers seem to require more sleep? Their bodies make more melatonin than someone older. As we age, our bodies produce less melatonin which can cause us to have more difficulty sleeping.

- Omega-3 fatty acids: These healthy fats are found in cold-water fish, flaxseed, flax oil, walnuts, and some other foods. Omega-3 supplements are being studied as a possible treatment for depression. More research is needed to determine if eating foods with omega-3 fatty acids can help relieve depression.

- Vitamin D: Dr. Weil, a well know holistic doctor suggests that a daily supplement of 2,000 or more mg. of vitamin D may help this condition. He says 70 percent of the U.S. population is deficient in vitamin D so it might be good in any case. This comes from his website, **www.drweil.com.**

Keep in mind that nutritional, and dietary products aren't monitored by the FDA. You can't always be sure of what you're getting and that it's safe. Also, because some herbal and dietary supplements can interfere with prescription medications or cause dangerous interactions, talk to your healthcare provider before taking any supplements.

More Steps to Prevent or Stop SAD

1. Get as much light into your life as you can.

2. Put up some full spectrum lighting.

3. Open the shades and sit by windows.

4. Get out and walk.

90

5. Take vitamin D. Look at suggestions in this chapter.

6. If your symptoms don't improve, go to the doctor and get help.

7. Not everyone can move to a sunny climate, so do what you need to do to stay healthy and energetic.

Get out of the dark and walk in the sun and you will find a reason to live.

11

Bullying

Alex, 14, Writes about Cyberbullying

Alex writes, "Children being cyberbullied can have self-esteem issues, confidence problems and even thoughts of suicide. It is important to work towards stopping cyber bullying because of the impact it can have. Cyberbullying adds another level of bullying to a child's mind.

Cyberbullying penetrates the barrier of a child's mind making him think he is not even safe from bullies at home. When I was around 14, I had a friend named Ryan. A kid named Liam was messing with him. Somehow Liam got hold of Ryan's cell phone number and was always sending cruel, harsh texts to him. Ryan was telling me how he couldn't seem to get a break. The poor guy always felt depressed and stressed at home. I suggested Ryan tell his parents, but he didn't want to because he felt embarrassed. I couldn't stand seeing Ryan like this so I decided to tell Ryan's parents. They got the whole thing taken care of quickly. My point is; kids don't need these kinds of problems at home. They should be able to feel safe and secure, not threatened; it can really mess with their heads."

Rebecca Sedwick Commits Suicide After Being Cyberbullied

[17] Rebecca Sedwick **jumped from a concrete silo tower** to her death on Sept. 9, 2013. This was reported by Polk County Sheriff Grady Judd. He brought two girls, ages 14 and 12, into custody because he saw a lack of remorse. He pointed to a Facebook post written Saturday night by the 14-year-old suspect, "Yes, I bullied Rebecca, and she killed herself, but I don't give a f---."

"You can add the last word yourself," Judd said. "We rushed the arrest because of their lack of remorse."

The bullying started in December 2012 when Rebecca and the two suspects were students at Crystal Lake Middle School, according to a statement from the Polk County Sheriff's Office.

"The girls sent Rebecca messages on Facebook calling her ugly, telling her to 'drink bleach and die,' and encouraging her to kill herself," Judd said.

Rebecca's parents tried to give her a fresh start at a new school in 2013-14. However, the torment continued online.

"Rebecca's family is absolutely devastated by this," Judd said. "Quite frankly, we're all devastated by this."

"Rebecca was a fragile child. Her parents separated her from the bullies, but she continued to be cyberbullied," said Judd. "When I stood at the base of that cement tower and saw the body of that twelve-year-old child it broke my heart. We are not putting up with this."

Reporting the Bully to Parents

When my daughter, Debi was 18 a boy at school called and left a message filled with nasty accusations and threats to cut off body parts. His remarks were recorded on our phone's answering machine. I was concerned about my daughter's safety, so I told her I was calling the police.

"I've already taken care of it, Mom," my daughter said, "I called his parents line and left his message on their phone. I don't think he is going to bother me anymore."

She was right. That boy never called our house again. But what about the kids, like Ryan, who are too ashamed to tell their parents or kids whose parents don't do anything?

Bullied All Through Grade School

From the time I was in the third grade until I finished the sixth grade, I was bullied by my classmates. On Valentine's Day, I received all skunk valentines except for the one the teacher gave me. On the playground, I was called names, kicked and abused physically. I was different than the other kids, so they attacked me verbally and sometimes physically.

We moved to the suburbs at the beginning of the third grade. My sister had eye surgery that year and had to be put back a grade. Not wanting to place us in a class together, they put me in a different class. The one I was moved to was one where the children had learning disabilities Being different I was mocked and put down. We had just moved from the inner city to the suburbs where we were a little behind. In the group they placed me in, I didn't learn to read above a second level and was never taught the multiplication tables. I thought something was wrong with me until I got into Jr. High where I became popular, but still struggled academically. I could have tried harder, but I assumed I was dumb. I had too much to do at home cleaning, cooking, and babysitting to do homework.

Freddie Prinze Jr. Was Bullied

Freddie Prinze committed suicide at the age of 22 in 1977. He was the star in "Chico and the Man" and loved by many. His son, Freddie Prinze Jr., is also a great actor. He talks about how it felt to be bullied by his peers. "I tried to step out of myself and somehow figure out how they were able to sleep at night calling me freak ….. or whatever their name of the week was. And I had to realize that was OK with them. It was something I was never able to do."

Most of us who would never deliberately bully another person cannot understand why people bully others. It makes no sense to us.

Mob Bullying

"Mobbing" is the bullying of an individual by a group such as a family, friends, peers, school, workplace, neighborhood, community, or online. One would think that bullying is just for kids and adults would not do that – but not true. In a family, it can be the "scapegoat": The child who gets blamed and punished for everything. The scapegoat is often bullied and mistreated by a sibling as well as the parents. "Ganging up" is emotional abuse on one person or child by family, co-workers, subordinates or superiors. The mental effects of mob bullying can be comparable with Post Traumatic Stress Disorder from war or prison camp experiences.

Patients may develop alcoholism or other substance abuse disorders. Family relationships routinely suffer. Some targets may even develop brief psychotic episodes, generally with paranoid symptoms. Sometimes the victim even considers suicide.

To Parents of Teens Being Bullied

1. Protect your child by letting the school and police know that your child is being bullied. Schools are no longer tolerating bullying.

2. Be active in your teen's life. Show up at events and parties.

3. Don't let your child's embarrassment stand in the way of their safety.

4. If social media is causing problems, don't allow it to be a part of your child's life. Many parents are choosing not to permit their teens on Facebook, for

example, to protect them from bullies and predators.

Action Steps If You Are Bullied

If you are being bullied, tell your parents; if this does not help talk to your school counselor! The bullying must stop!

Remember, you have a reason to live, and no one has the right to define who you are except your creator.

12

Suicide in Colleges and Universities

Suicide is the Second Leading Cause of Death for College Students

Suicide is the second leading cause of death in college students. Think of all the changes a college student goes through, particularly if they are living away from home. They probably still feel the loss of family and friends. Suddenly they're alone and isolated with no one to talk to. They face new challenges and expectations. Fear of failure can overwhelm them. College students are also concerned at times about finances. Being overwhelmed, lonely and away from family and friends can cause depression. Fact: one-half of all college students say they felt so depressed they found it difficult to function in the past year.

One in Ten College Students Has Considered Suicide

Depression, loneliness, and new expectations can cause a college student to feel overwhelmed and afraid they cannot fulfill all that is required of them. One friend can make a big difference in the life of a college student who is dealing with loneliness. That feeling of inadequacy and stress can overwhelm a student. These feelings can lead to depression. Untreated depression is one of the leading causes of suicide.

Chemical Changes in the Body of a Young Person

College students are also coming to the age when they can notice for the first time seasonal affective disorder, SAD. Usually, this is not experienced in those who are younger than 18 but the long cloudy winters and short days can affect the mood and cause depression. When it's a chemical imbalance, such as SAD, it can be helped with antidepressants and light therapy. Other chemical imbalances may also show up in the college years. Schizophrenia usually occurs with young men in their twenties. Bipolar disorder is another chemical imbalance that could appear in the college years. Borderline personality is an imbalance where medication and counseling may be needed. Don't hesitate to get help if you feel an imbalance is occurring in your body.

[18]Why is the Suicide Rate So High Among College Students?

In a recent study on college-age suicide made by Johns Hopkins Children's Center, the University of Maryland and other institutions more than one-thousand students were interviewed from a mid-Atlantic university throughout their four-year college careers. A team of researchers asked each student in-depth questions about his or her background and thoughts on suicide. While twelve percent of the group admitted they had thought about committing suicide, ten percent of them claimed to have planned or attempted suicide during college.

The study's findings suggest that some common risk factors may make students more prone to suicidal tendencies. The greatest of these factors is a feeling of being unloved or detached from friends and family. The research pointed to other factors as well, including having symptoms of depression or having a mother with depression, as well as having been abused or having witnessed abuse during childhood.

Helping Each Other

Colorado State University President, Tony Frank, sent out a note to all students after two eighteen-year-old freshmen were found in their dorms after committing suicide. "Ask for help when you're hurting," Frank wrote to students. "Take care of yourselves and each other. Tell someone when you have concerns for a friend who's struggling. Understand and never forget that you are important and have value, not just to your families and our University community but to our world." [19]

What College Students Need to Prevent Depression and Suicidal Thoughts

Last year, three undergraduates from Cornell committed suicide. Another from Yale leaped from the top of the Empire State Building. Why?

For every student who commits suicide, dozens have attempted it unsuccessfully, and thousands have thought about it. Depression, discouragement and psychological distress that college students face are seldom reported.

Many colleges do not have a counseling center where students can go for help.

The more naïve and sheltered students are, the more likely they are to feel overwhelmed, lonely, confused and depressed. They may not be prepared for the temptations they face on campus. Going to college isn't just about attending a new academic institution. It's a barrage of change and novelty. There are new friends, a new city, new living quarters, new roommates, new food, new schedules, new social milieu, and distance from the old network of social support.

Nothing has prepared them for this, even if their high school had "college preparatory" in its name. Parents are in a position to ease that stress, helping smooth the transition to college. Or at the very least, they can catch the trouble before it gets out of hand.

Change is stressful, even if it is a positive change. Let's face it, when a young person who has been sheltered goes to college, he or she is cut off from their old support system. If they have even one person they can talk to that encourages them, it can keep them from being overwhelmed. But often when they do get involved with someone, it may be a romantic situation that can distract them and even break their heart. They can easily get distracted from making good grades which can cause depression. A student can get into a downward spiral without knowing where to turn for help.

There are Christian organizations on many college campuses that will supply support such as "Young Life" and "Campus Crusade for Christ."

Making the Grade

Most students who go to college have high expectations of doing well. In the midst of a positive life change, grades may not be as high as they expected. You may want to avoid challenging classes that first year while you are adjusting to college life. My grandson recently graduated from high school and is now in college. Although he graduated at the top of his class and is considering becoming a doctor, he has chosen to go to a junior college his first year. In this way, he can still keep his grades up without going through the adjustment of being separated from home and family. He also goes to a church where he receives support and encouragement.

Romance: Many eighteen-year-old college freshmen are inexperienced in romantic relationships. With all the extreme emotions that go with a romantic involvement, it may cause distractions from academic success and trauma if it fails. Depression, grief, and loss may occur when a young student has a "break up" with their boy or girlfriend. Feelings of depression can lead to more serious thoughts of suicide. This is the time to get some help from friends, church, and family.

Alcohol and drugs: Drug and alcohol use on campus is real. Even those who didn't previously drink or use drugs find it easy to get involved with them being away from home and with peers.

I had a journalism professor that met with students in a bar every evening. They talked and drank. I met with them one time but realized that I would not be able to keep my grades up if I did that on a regular basis. It was a way for some of the students to get support, but anything in excess can be harmful.

Reach Out!

Students that feel overwhelmed by the temptations, losses, stresses, and expectations of campus life and feel depressed and suicidal may call **1-800-SUICIDE**.

It is a grave mistake to believe that you can manage depression on your own. You cannot treat any other illness by yourself, so don't think you should deal with depression alone. To learn more about depression and suicide go to **www.suicide.org**. Read as much as possible, and if you think that you need help, call!

Again, if you feel depressed, please get help **immediately**. Your "Blues" may not seem like a big deal now, but depression can worsen, and quickly cause suicidal feelings. If you are depressed, make appointments to see a doctor and/or a therapist. If you are low on funds, try to find a low-cost clinic. Some colleges have "Student Services" that are free or cost little. Check them out. Get help when you need it. And remember that it is not weakness, but a sign of strength to reach out for help.

Action Steps for College Students

1. If you are in college and feel overwhelmed and depressed let your parents know what you are going through.

2. If your college has a Student Services clinic, contact them and make an appointment.
3. If you have a friend to talk to, this is the time to call them.
4. Don't isolate!
5. Get rid of sources, you have thought of using, to harm yourself.
6. You have a future and hope. Don't give up! You have only just begun.
7. Tell yourself, "Suicide is not an Option" over and over again.

Action Steps for Parents: Stay in touch with your child. Take their depression seriously. Do whatever you have to do to help them break the cycle of depression.

A reason to live: I just read a book by a father whose 22-year-old son committed suicide. The title of it was "The Hope Of Heaven" by Alan Haller and Erin Marshall. The devastation family and friends would go through with your suicide is beyond any problems you might be facing right now. Your problems are temporary. Death is permanent.

13

When Evil People Drive Others to Suicide

Parents Give Son a Deadly Christmas Present

[20]In the book, *People of the Lie*, Dr. Scott Peck describes a couple whose sixteen-year-old son, Stuart, committed suicide with a .22 caliber rifle. The following Christmas, the parents, gave their fifteen-year-old son, Bobby the same gun his brother had committed suicide with the previous summer.

Dr. Peck describes a counseling session with the parents of Bobby. "I'm concerned about the Christmas present you gave Bobby," Peck said.

"Christmas present?" The parents seemed confused.

"Yes. I understand you gave him a rifle," said Peck

"That's right."

"Was that what he asked for?"

"How should I know what he asked for," the father demanded belligerently. Then immediately his matter turned plaintiff. "I can't remember what he asked for. A lot

has happened to us, you know. This has been a hard year for us."

"I believe it has been," Peck said, "but why did you give him a gun?"

"Why? Why not? It's a good present for a boy his age. Most kids his age would give their eyeteeth for a gun," the father said.

"I should think," Peck said slowly, "that since your other son killed himself with a rifle that you wouldn't feel so kindly toward them." "

"You are one of those anti-gun people, aren't you?" the father asked faintly belligerent again. "Well, that's all right. You can be that way. I'm no gun nut myself, but it does seem to me that guns aren't the problem it's the people who use them."

"To an extent, I agree with you," Peck said. "Stuart didn't kill himself simply because he had a gun. There must've been some other reason more important. Do you know what that reason might have been?"

"No. We've already told you we didn't even know that Stuart was depressed."

"That's right. Stuart was depressed." Peck said. "People don't commit suicide unless they're depressed. Since you didn't know Stuart was despondent, there was perhaps no reason for you to worry about him having a gun. But you

did know Bobby was depressed. You knew he was in that state well before Christmas, well before you gave him the gun."

"Please, doctor, you don't seem to understand," the mother said, taking over her husband. "We really didn't know it was this serious. We just thought he was upset because of his brother."

"So you gave him his brother's suicide weapon. Not just any gun; but that particular one!"

The father took the lead again. "We couldn't afford to get him a new one. I don't know why you're picking on us. We gave him the best present we could. Money doesn't grow on trees, you know. We are just ordinary working people. We could have sold the gun and made money. But we didn't. We kept it so we could give Bobby a nice present."

"Did you think how that present might not seem 'right' to Bobby?" Peck asked.

"No, we didn't think about that. We're not educated people like you," pleaded the mother. "We haven't been to college and learned all kinds of fancy ways of thinking. We're just simple working people. We can't be expected to think of all these things."

"Perhaps not," Peck said. "That's what worries me because this stuff needs to be thought of."

107

Were The Parents Evil or Stupid?

Dr. Peck recommended Bobby go live with his aunt and uncle. He did very well living with them while continuing his counseling. Most people would not think of this couple as evil. But when you look at them giving their son the gun his older brother killed himself with, it appears they were either stupid or evil. I think they were evil because when they were confronted with the knowledge that their actions could cause Bobby to commit suicide, they showed no remorse.

Heroes That Stood Against Evil

Most of us think of people like Hitler as evil. When Hitler took power, he was praised as a god who had come to save Germany. There were those like the Ten Boom family and Dietrich Bonhoeffer, who knew he was evil. But the majority of people did not see Hitler that way. Bonhoeffer was a Lutheran pastor who saw Hitler taking over the churches. He gave his life to put a stop to Hitler's rule. *"Agent of Grace"* is a movie showing Bonhoeffer's commitment to God and his battle against Hitler. When the Nazi's heard the American bombs in the distance, they put many of the prisoners to death. Bonhoeffer was hung just weeks before our troops took over Germany.

The Ten Boom family took in the Jews. For that crime, most of the Ten Boom family members were murdered. Casper Ten Boom, the father of the family, said when the Germans were persecuting the Jewish people, "I pity them,

Corrie, (his daughter), they have touched the apple of God's eye."

Individuals who Commit Suicide are Seldom Evil

In centuries past, people thought anyone who killed themselves was evil. That was true in some cases. Hitler committed suicide. But most suicides are not done by such people. They are people driven to suicide by emotional or physical pain, grief, hopeless life situations or chemical imbalances, such as those with bipolar disorder, schizophrenia, etc. And there were some driven to the point of suicide by evil people.

Some such cruel people are in our prisons and psychiatric wards, but many are in critical positions in the community. Such a person can live right next door or work with you at the office. Evil people are often in powerful positions.

Wealthy Lawyer Seeks to Destroy Wife and Children

Damien was a well to do lawyer who inherited a lot of money from his successful father. He grew up in wealth and luxury. He married a sweet, gentle woman, Gloria and had a son and a daughter, Gary, and Jenny. His wife loved them more than anything in the world.

Damien decided to leave his wife so he could be free to date other women but had one problem. He had no intention of paying child support or permitting his wife to have custody of the children. Systematically this man sought to drive his wife to suicide. He convinced her to sign herself into the psychiatric ward of the hospital. After she had followed his advice, it was easy to get custody with proof that she was unstable and had to be hospitalized. Being a lawyer, he was able to do this. For her to see the children every other weekend, she had to pay child support to her wealthy ex-husband. She had to move in with her mother to cover the expenses. Few people saw him as evil. Most thought his ex-wife was an unstable, suicidal alcoholic. Evil is deceitful!

He began seeing another young lady who had two children of her own. Joyce made a good salary. She wanted a stable family with dinners around the table and security. It appeared Damien with his two children could provide that. Before she could fully see his manipulation, deceit, and lies, he rushed her into marriage. By the time, she realized how evil he really was she was pregnant. "I felt forever trapped with a controlling, manipulating, cold, calculating man," she said.

After her baby, Sally was born she hoped to stay home with her for a while, but he forced to go back to work. She decided to end the marriage when she discovered Damien was having sex with prostitutes. He spent long hours developing one evil scheme after another to destroy Joyce emotionally, financially and physically. Although very wealthy, this man sought to take everything she had, including their young daughter. Through all the court hearings and costs, he made sure that she was financially destitute. But she was able to get joint custody of their

110

daughter. After the divorce, he continued to hire prostitutes.

What is Evil?

Evil doesn't always appear to be "evil." Evil can come, seemingly as kindness and love. Evil knows how to deceive. The Bible tells us that Satan is evil and the author of lies and deception.

What is evil? Evil is often thought of as murder, rape, or genocide. What does God say is evil? There are seven things God hates, (or says are evil). (Proverbs 6:16-19 - NLT)

- *Haughty eyes*
- *A lying tongue*
- *Hands that kill the innocent*
- *A heart that plots evil*
- *A false witness who pours out lies*
- *Feet that race to do wrong*
- *A person who sows discord in a family*

Those who have been raped, battered emotionally and/or physically and bullied have a higher rate of suicide. Evil people seek to control others. According to Dr. Scott Peck, "Evil is the force, residing either inside or outside of human beings, that wants to kill life or liveliness. And goodness is its opposite. Goodness is that which promotes life and liveliness."[21]

Evil is *LIVE* spelled backward — *EVIL*. It is the opposite of what brings life. Put a 'D' in front of the word evil, and you have *Devil*. Putting it simply, God is the creator of life; the Devil seeks to kill and destroy. Evil destroys the spirit as well as the body. The desire of some people to control others can actually destroy them.

Love is the opposite of evil. The Bible has a beautiful description of love. *"Love is very patient and kind, never jealous or envious, never boastful or proud, never haughty or selfish or rude. Love does not demand its own way. It is not irritable or touchy. It does not hold grudges and will hardly even notice when others do it wrong. It is never glad about injustice but rejoices whenever truth wins out. If you love someone, you will be loyal to him no matter what the cost. You will always believe in him, always expect the best of him, and always stand your ground in defending him."* (1Corinthians 13:4-7 LB)

Where does evil come from? How does one become evil? The Bible says, *"He did evil because he had not set his heart on seeking the Lord."* (2 Chronicles 12:14 NIV)

[22]When we think of evil we think of history's tyrannical rulers and dictators, we think of mass murders, cannibals, and humanity twisted into psychological monsters of crime against the innocent. It is a shock to see the definition of evil in this scripture as being simply that a man "did not set his heart on seeking the Lord."

112

Evil is the opposite of what the Bible calls good. Jesus took the Ten Commandments and simplified them down to two commandments. Love God and love others. If you love God and love others, you will not be lying, stealing and being disrespectful of others. The Bible also talks about light and darkness. Evil is darkness. Good is light. Light is Truth. Darkness is a lie.

While working at the Juvenile Court, I talked with a father whose 16-year-old daughter was depressed and suicidal. Her father described her as rebellious and in need of being broken. As I listened to all his rules, his home sounded more like a prison than a safe place to live. I encouraged him to sit down with his wife and daughter and come up with rules they could all agree on. Shocked he said, "If I do that, she will win."

"If someone in the family loses, the whole family loses," I told him. "A nurturing loving family knows how to make everyone a winner."

Love is not worried about winning. Love wants the beloved to win. In a loving family, everyone wins. The goal is to nurture, care and give life and love to each family member. It is not to beat down, control, deceive, manipulate or hurt anyone in the household.

A year later the mother and daughter visited me at work to tell me they had left the father and were happy and free.

Evil in the Media

A rainy cold Thursday night on September 15, 1977, Jack and Rosemary Kirkham got a knock on their door. A police chaplain came to tell them that their four grandchildren had been murdered: Steve 14, Greg 12, Tonya 3 and Stacy 17 months. Billy Dyer 14, a Junior High boy had watched the movie, *Helter Skelter* about Charles Manson and wanted to know what it felt like to kill someone.

In 1984, a 19-year-old boy shot himself in the head and died while he was listening to Ozzy Osbourne sing the song, "Suicide Solution." The lyrics: "....where to hide, suicide, is the only way out. Don't you know what it's really about?"

A group of four mothers formed the PMRC, which stands for, Parents Music Resource Center in 1985. The PMRC felt that the lyrics were getting so bad that the parents should be warned. Today in the bottom corner of the cover of CD's there are warning labels saying, "**warning explicit lyrics**" meaning the words may have bad language or content. Too many bands play music with lyrics that talk about suicide, sex, drug abuse, and violence.

We parents, grandparents, and caregivers need to be more aware of the things to which our youth are watching and listening.

Action Steps: If you realize you are being influenced by evil get away from it. If someone is trying to convince you to hurt yourself or continually putting you down, get away from them. Let them know that you will not tolerate it. If you are listening to music, watching movies or playing games that make you think of suicide; STOP! Protect your mind from evil!

Action Steps For Parents and Caregivers: If your children are being influenced by evil. Get them away from the source!

Reason To Live: Most people are not evil. Surround yourself with those who are nurturing and caring. Your life is unique. God has a plan for you. Focus on God and fulfill your destiny. Don't give evil people the power to destroy you.

14

Religion and Suicide

Medieval Christian laws concerning suicide were cruel. They were a combination of prohibitions and old superstitions concerning the troubled and restless soul. The body of a person who committed suicide was dramatically and publicly abused. They ran stakes through the heart of the deceased. The body was buried at a busy crossroad. The family estates of those who committed suicide were confiscated. If someone attempted suicide, they were punished. Christians, Jews, and Moslems have historically condemned suicide, saying it deliberately destroys one's life and denies the divine will of God.

Great Men of the Bible Who Despaired of Life

King Solomon was anointed by God to be the wisest man who ever lived. He wrote most of the books of Proverbs, Song of Songs and Ecclesiastes. His pursuit of pleasure reached the point where he said, *"I hated life because the work that is done under the sun is grievous to me. All of it is meaningless."* (Eccl; 2:17). Elijah was one of the greatest prophets in the Bible. After God had given him the power to perform a great miracle, he became fearful, depressed and yearned for death, he prayed, *"I have had enough, Lord. Take my life..."* (I Kings 19:4). Jonah, the prophet, was so angry at God that he wished to die, saying,

"It would be better for me to die than to live." (Jonah 4:8). Even the Apostle Paul and his missionary companions at one point became so discouraged he wrote, *"We think you ought to know, dear brothers and sisters, about the trouble we went through in the province of Asia. We were crushed and overwhelmed beyond our ability to endure, and we thought we would never live through it."* (2 Cor. 1:8 NLT).

None of these men committed suicide. Solomon learned to *"fear God and keep his commandments, for this is the duty of all mankind"* (Eccl. 12:13). Elijah was comforted by an angel, allowed to rest, and given a new commission. Jonah received admonition and rebuke from God, (along with another chance). Paul learned that although the pressure he faced was beyond his ability to endure, the Lord can bear all things: *"This happened that we might not rely on ourselves but on God, who raises the dead,"* (2 Cor. 1:9).

Is Suicide the Unforgivable Sin?

Suicide is a sin, but not the unforgivable sin. It has a damaging and lasting effect on those left behind. The painful scars left by such a death do not quickly heal. *"May God grant His grace to each one who is facing trials today."* (Psalm 67:1). May each of us find hope in the promise, *"Everyone who calls on the name of the Lord will be saved,"* (Rom. 10:13).

Some ministers refuse to conduct a funeral for someone who has committed suicide. Some see suicide as an unforgivable sin and refuse to help anyone who is suicidal. What do men like Billy Graham and Max Lucado have to

117

say? Many of the great leaders in the Bible and of our day suffered depression and hopelessness. Even Jesus experienced despair in the garden of Gethsemane. Jesus said to his disciples, "My soul is overwhelmed to the point of death. Stay here and keep watch with me." He went back in the garden and prayed, *"My Father, if it is possible may this cup be taken from me. Yet not as I will, but as you will."* (Matt. 26:39)

Freddie Prinze was a young comedian and good actor. He played Chico in *Chico and the Man*. Prinze was arrested on November 16, 1976, for driving under the influence of Quaaludes, (a sedative, hypnotic drug). A few weeks later his wife Kathy Elaine Prinze filed for divorce saying he was endangering the life of his baby son, Freddie Prize Jr., with his drug use. Prinze suffered extreme depression from the rejection. His business manager, Marvin "Dusty" Snyder got a call from Prinze that concerned him so much he went over to his apartment to encourage him. Prinze called his mother saying, "Mom, I love you very much, but I can't go on. I need to find peace."

He called his estranged wife saying, "I love you, Kathy. I love the baby, but I need to find peace. I can't go on." With his manager looking on Prinze put a gun to his head and shot himself. He died at 1:00 pm. on January 29, 1977, at the age of 22.

I was a young housewife living in the suburbs when I heard of Freddie Prinze's suicide. Some people I considered good Christians were saying, "Prinze is in hell because he committed suicide."

118

I started asking God to show me the truth. Was Prinze in hell because he committed suicide? As I prayed, a vision of Jesus holding young Prinze came to my mind with Jesus saying, "Some are not strong enough to endure the trials of earth."

Prinze carried his Bible with him everywhere and talked to God in his diary. In his Bible, he wrote, "Dear Lord, I am not afraid to die. But please let me live until I buy my mom the house I promised her."

He was a lonely kid. After he married Kathy he thought, there would be less loneliness. When she chose to divorce him, he was devastated. His doctor had put him on Quaaludes, which have since been outlawed. A manager he had fired was suing him. Although he was very successful for a 22-year-old, he had more loneliness, fear, and worries than most that age.

I briefly mentioned the book "The Hope Of Heaven," back in Chapter 12, (Suicide in Colleges and Universities), My vision was like the vision the father, Hallen Jr., had as he held his 22-year-old son who hung himself. In his book, he wrote of the encouragement he received from God after he found his son's body. "The bad decisions a Christ-follower makes do affect life on earth, and we will face accountability for them in heaven." (2 Cor. 5:10), *"For we must all stand before Christ to be judged. We will each receive whatever we deserve for the good or evil we have done in this earthly body. But no one who seeks the Lord as Savior is ever lost to Him.*

What Does Billy Graham Say about Suicide?

[23]**Question:** My sister struggled with severe depression most of her life and had to be hospitalized several times. Last year, she got so depressed she took her own life. In spite of everything, she had a strong faith. Is suicide the unforgivable sin, as some people say? It's all been very painful to me.

Answer: *The only sin God cannot forgive is the sin of rejecting the Holy Spirit's witness to Jesus Christ and His offer of forgiveness. Only when we reject God will He reject us. This alone is the unforgivable "blasphemy against the Spirit" of which Jesus spoke* (Matt. 12:31).

God understands your heartache, and I want to assure you that He also knew all about your sister's struggles. Medical science has made many advances in helping us understand emotional problems, but there's still much we don't understand. Take confidence in your sister's faith in Christ, and rejoice that she is now beyond the pains and sorrows of this world.

I don't want to be misunderstood, however. Suicide is severe and tragic in God's eyes, and if someone who is reading this is contemplating suicide, I beg of you to reconsider and seek help for whatever your problem may be. God loves you whether you believe it or not – and He does not want you to end your life. Satan does, however, and you must not listen to him

Instead, put your faith and hope in Christ and His love for you. You are never alone if you know Him because nothing "will be able to separate us from the love of God that is in Christ Jesus our Lord" **(Rom. 8:39).**

[24]**Question**: My cousin had significant emotional problems most of her life, and finally they overwhelmed her, and she committed suicide. I firmly believe she was a Christian but did she lose her salvation by doing this? Is suicide the unpardonable sin?

Answer: *Whenever I answer a question like this, I'm deeply aware that someone may be reading this who is seriously contemplating suicide—and I would do everything in my power to convince them not to take that final, drastic step. With Christ, there is always hope.*

God loves them; He loves them so much that Jesus Christ was willing to die on the cross for their salvation. And others care about them, as well, (even if they have a hard time believing it). Suicide is never God's will, and even in the midst of life's worst storms we can look to Christ and discover that He truly is "…an anchor for the soul, firm and secure" (Hebrews 6:19)*. The first step back from the brink of suicide is to turn to Christ and open our hearts to Him.*

Suicide is always a tragedy—but in itself, it is not the unpardonable sin. The only sin God cannot pardon is the sin of rejecting Him. God knew your cousin's heart, and He also knew that mental illness sometimes clouds a person's judgment so much that they aren't entirely responsible for their actions.

At the same time, ask God to help you be sensitive to the needs of others—especially someone who may be facing discouragement or depression. Often just knowing that someone cares will help them turn the corner.

Great Christian Leaders Who Battled Depression and Suicide

Some great Christian leaders were suicidality depressed.

Samuel Logan Brengle; Salvation Army's most influential teacher and author of books on Holiness battled severe bouts of depression. "My nerves were ragged, frazzled, exhausted. And such gloom and depression fell upon me as I have never known. God seemed nonexistent. The grave seemed my endless goal. Life lost all of its glory, charm, and meaning. Prayer brought me no relief. I had lost the spirit and power of prayer."

J. B. Phillips, author, and Bible translator wrote, "I found that I could usually struggle on pretty well during the day. But at night, it was as if I were the chosen target of the Enemy. Irrational fears gripped my spirit, unreal guilt swept over me. Even my sense of God disappeared though it never reached nihilism or utter despair. Still, when I turned to God for help, He seemed remote and unapproachable."

[25]C. H. Spurgeon a nineteenth-century revivalist and one of the greatest preachers in history, in 1866 told his congregation, "I am subject to depression of spirit so

fearful I hope none of you ever gets to such extremes of wretchedness as I go to."

Tragedy struck Spurgeon on October 19, 1856, as he was preaching at the Surrey Gardens Music Hall for the first time. Someone in the crowd yelled, "Fire!" The ensuing panic and stampede left several dead. Spurgeon was emotionally devastated by the event, and it had a significant influence on his life. He struggled with depression for many years and spoke of being moved to tears for no reason known to him.

William Cowper, an English poet who wrote great hymns such as, *There is a Fountain* and *O for a Closer Walk with God*, experienced mental sickness off and on from the age of twenty till his death at sixty-nine. He experienced a period of depression and insanity causing him to attempt suicide three times. He was sent to Nathaniel Cotton's asylum at St. Albans for recovery. He wrote his greatest hymn, *God Moves in a Mysterious Way*, after an attack of insanity during which he tried to drown himself.

Great men in history that loved God have battled depression. David Brainerd was a missionary to the American Indians, who suffered physical and mental pain throughout his life. He died at the age of 29 from tuberculosis. Another example is F.B. Meyer, an outstanding preacher, leader, and writer whose books still sell well decades after his death. After serving God fruitfully for many years, he experienced a period of nine years in which he lived in deep darkness and depression, wondering if he even belonged to the Lord at all. Some of the greatest men that have ever lived and given their lives to God and others have battled despair, depression, and suicide.

Jeremiah was a prophet and great man of God. Yet he wrote:

"Cursed be the day I was born! May the day my mother bore me not be blessed! [15] Cursed be the man who brought my father the news, who made him very glad saying, "A child is born to you a son" [16] May that man be like the towns the LORD overthrew without pity. May he hear wailing in the morning, a battle cry at noon. [17] For he did not kill me in the womb, with my mother as my grave, her womb enlarged forever. [18] Why did I ever come out of the womb to see trouble and sorrow to end my days in shame?" (Jer. 20:13-18, NIV)

Paul wrote, *"While we live in these earthly bodies, we groan and sigh, but it's not that we want to die and get rid of these bodies that clothe us. Rather, we want to put on our new bodies so that these dying bodies will be swallowed up by life."* (2 Cor. 5:4, NLT).

Jesus had told his disciple before he was crucified, *"My soul is crushed with grief to the point of death. Stay here and keep watch with me. He went on a little farther and bowed with his face to the ground, praying, "My Father! If it is possible, let this cup of suffering be taken away from me. Yet I want your will to be done, not mine.",* (Matt. 26:38-40 NLT)

As long as we are human beings in these broken bodies, living in an imperfect world, we can suffer despair and depression even to the point of wishing we were never born or wanting to die.

Max Lucado's Compassionate Views on Suicide

[26]"Suicide victims battled life's rawest contests. They often faced a mental illness or diseases and felt the peril of mental fatigue. What you and I take for granted, they coveted. Optimism; Hope; Confidence that all would be well. Their clouds had no silver linings; their storms had no rainbows.

Didn't we wonder why couldn't he snap out of this slump and shrug off this case of the blues, buck up and move forward? Of course, had the struggle been a physical one, we wouldn't have asked those questions. Of cancer patients, we don't ask, "Why didn't they get rid of that melanoma?" We understand the power of cancer. We may not understand the mystery of mental illness. I certainly don't. But this much I have observed. Depression can cause people to make the wrong choice.

Let's be clear: suicide is the wrong choice. The date of our death is God's to choose, not ours. He gives life and he takes it. When people orchestrate their own death, they make the wrong choice.

But is the mistake a spiritually fatal one? Do we despair of any hope of their eternal salvation? Are we left with the nightmarish conclusion that heaven holds no place for them? By no means! While suicide is the wrong choice, have we not all made bad choices? And did Christ not come for people like us? Frame their lives rightly. Remember their good, even great decisions. Jesus said, *"Come to me, all you who labor and are heavy laden, and I*

125

will give you rest" (Matt. 11:28 NKJV). God does not measure a person by one decision, nor should we."

Max Lucado Shares Words of Hope for Those Who Battle Depression and Thoughts of Suicide

Linda Evans Shepard interviewed the pastor Max Lucado for the website, *www.thinkingaboutsuicide.com.*[27] "The message of grace is pertinent for those who are in tough times because it takes the burden off of the person and places the burden on God. Grace says that salvation and strength are God based, God-given, God-driven," said Lucado. "Every other religion and philosophy in the world says that it's up to us to get God's attention or to win God's favor—but Grace says, '**No!** You already have God's attention. You already have God's favor."

"Those who are passing through times of despair feel as though they can relate to the orphan because they feel like nobody really cares. But the theme of grace is that God does not just pat us on the back, he gives us a place at his table. He gives us His name; He brings us into His family because He has made us His children. His act of adopting us once and for all declares – I must be worth something. I must have hope and a future."

Knowing that God gives us a future and a hope, as well as the courage to go on in painful times, should be a great comfort to all of us.

126

Confession the Key to Release of Unresolved Guilt by Max Lucado

"After thirty years as a pastor, I believe most people carry around unresolved guilt;" said Lucado. "A regret or a failure—and they've never talked to God about it. Satan uses guilt because the commodity of Satan is condemnation. Satan wakes up every day wanting to figure out a way to make us feel guilty. The Bible calls him the accuser and his goal is to condemn us and to create within us a feeling of condemnation. If we learn to confess quickly, 'Lord, I'm sorry for what I did. I accept your grace,' then we would live in a state of confession, not in a state of guilt. To live in a state of receiving this forgiveness of God, all you have to say is, 'Lord, I'm sorry, please forgive me.' Then, confess precisely what you did; 'I looked at a woman in the wrong way. I spoke out of turn, …….' "

Max explained, "On the days I actually apply this, I find myself practicing dozens of confessions. But it's not a sense in which I'm just beating myself up, it's a constant conversation that takes place in the back of my mind, between God and me and it's so liberating! Then there's the issue of these deep-seated poor choices we made years ago that have never been dealt with. Many people need to go back and have a good talk with God about that: About the night or the time in the back seat of a car, with the drugs or the abortion. Some of these major issues we've never really let God forgive."

127

Action Steps:

1. Let go of past mistakes and sins.
2. Talk with God about those areas you have kept hidden in a dark place in your heart.
3. Bring them to God and let Him cleanse your heart from all past and present sins.

15

Suicide in the Military

Appreciation for Members of Our Military

A young soldier sat at a table across from Richard and me at a Cracker Barrel Restaurant. He sat alone. *"Thank the young soldier,"* a voice in my mind said.

I knew the voice. It was God speaking to my heart. *"But I don't know this soldier,"* I argued. *"It will be embarrassing to go over to his table and thank him when I don't know him."*

It doesn't matter what I think when God is telling me to do something. I got up and walked over to his table. **"Sir, I want to thank you for your service to our country. I appreciate what you are doing,"** I said.

"No one has ever said that to me before. You have no idea what that means to me. I just got back from Afghanistan," he said.

I knew I had done the right thing as I sat back down at our table. When Richard and I got ready to get our bill, the waitress said, "There is no charge. The young soldier that sat across from you paid your bill."

Shocked I thought, "**Millions of young men and women in the military have paid our bill. They paid for our FREEDOM.**"

More Deaths from Suicide Than in Combat

There are more deaths by suicide among those who served in Iraq and Afghanistan than those who died in battle. Government statistics show an average of 22 veterans a day die from suicide. This is most likely far below the actual numbers. Only 21 states participated in the survey with 34,000 suicides discarded because the state failed to put the deceased was a veteran, on the death certificate. Suicides are under-reported. Senator Joe Donnelly of Indiana reported that 349 servicemembers committed suicide, which is more than the 295 killed in combat in Afghanistan. Suicide attempts along with Post-traumatic Stress Disorder cases are not all reported.[28]

The trauma our service members and their families have endured is not shown in statistics. Many suicide attempts of those in the military as well as family members have never been recorded. The trauma of what our military families go through is beyond our comprehension.

Shortage of Mental Health Professionals in the VA System

There is a shortage of mental health professionals in the VA system to help veterans. Those men and women who do try to get help often find there is a nationwide shortage of mental health care professionals which causes long lines and waits for appointments. [29]

Because of this shortage, the military should set up a system of "Veterans Helping Veterans." People who have been through the trauma of deployment and war could be trained to come alongside a vet who has been traumatized by their service in the military, to counsel and work with them. Veterans could be taught to understand and help each other. A trained veteran could be assigned to someone waiting for an appointment with a specialist. They could be that one safe person the vet could talk to, knowing he has a comrade who understands his struggles.

Suicides by Vietnam Veterans

My seven-year-old granddaughter and I were shopping when we saw a Vietnam vet in a wheelchair. He had no legs and was asking for money. I pulled out a $10 bill and gave it to him. My granddaughter was shocked that I gave him money. "Why did you do that Gramma?"

"Sweetheart, you have no idea what that young man, who went to Vietnam, went through. He sacrificed his legs for our freedom. We need to help them in any way we can. Those men have suffered more than most of us can ever begin to understand."

Suicide rates among Vietnam veterans are the highest of any group, according to John Draper, project director of the National Suicide Prevention Lifeline.[30] Soldiers throughout the ages have suffered injuries and trauma due to the horrors of war. Their personal beliefs about right and wrong, conscience, compassion, and humanity are shattered, after seeing young children and women slaughtered.

Some were forced to kill whole villages. They saw the Vietnam children laughing and playing. They saw women crying. No matter how hard they tried to believe what they were forced to do was right, in their minds, it was still wrong. So they became filled with extreme mental anguish and guilt. There was no way they could make it fit their strong beliefs to protect the innocent. During the Vietnam War young men were drafted unless they had children or were in college. Young men who were drafted and forced to go to Vietnam were often called *baby killers.*

Suicide Attempts by Family Members of Men/Women in the Military

When I worked as a Family Support Worker with Navy families, two young mothers who were pregnant on my caseload attempted suicide when their husbands were deployed in 1999 to 2001. The families I counseled had young children or were getting ready to have a baby. I worked closely with those whose mates were being deployed. Both mothers who attempted suicide were pregnant with their second child. Family members were high risk for suicide. Unfortunately, no records are kept on how many of these deaths occur with family remembers of service men.

It is important that military families get the support they need. Most of the families I worked with were living on poverty level wages along with having their mates being deployed. Some bases have houses on the site so wives and children can get together and support each other. The families I worked with did not live on base. They were isolated from their peers and separated from their families.

Sophie 28 sought an abortion even though she and her husband wanted a baby. She cried to me saying, "I can't have a baby when my family is all in California, and we are here in Texas. I need my family."

I encouraged her to get an ultrasound before making any final decision. My phone rang a few nights later with Sophie on the other end saying, "Patricia, you must come over and see our baby girl."

I drove over to her apartment, and she joyously showed me pictures of the ultrasound. "Isn't she beautiful," she said. "My family will come from California to help when she is born."

Jenny 20 had a cesarean (surgery), to deliver her baby girl. Her husband was deployed at the time, and she was suicidal with postpartum depression and psychosis. Isolated, Jenny had no contact with the outside world, except with me. Her mother died when she was twelve, and she had no family except her husband and the new baby. Jenny kept getting flashbacks of her mother's death after coming home to an empty house. She did not know how to get out of the pain she was in except through suicide. I sat for hours with her, letting her cry and pour out the grief Jenny had never been able to share with anyone. She had buried these feelings, and when the baby came, they were all coming out at once. When we were able to get through some of the grief of her childhood, another crisis surfaced.

She found emails on the computer showing her husband was having an affair with another lady on his ship. So she suffered postpartum depression, isolation and eventually a divorce from being the wife of a Navy Officer. It is not uncommon for a young man or woman to have an affair on the ship.

Several of the mothers I worked with dealt with isolation and depression. Even though records are not kept of family members, who have attempted suicide, I am sure from my experience with families dealing with poverty, isolation, and lack of support that many were depressed to the point of killing themselves. I don't think most of the military bases have Social Workers that visit the homes of young families with babies and small children. Many of the women who needed my help couldn't even get out to get into a support group. Two young ladies, I worked with were being abused by their husbands. Amy, 17, had a twelve-month-old baby boy and was pregnant. She didn't drive, so the only people she saw were her husband and me. Her depression increased until she was suicidal and could admit her husband was abusive. We got her into a battered women's shelter and contacted her parents. They were able to come and stay with her. The Navy supplied anger management classes for her husband.

[31]The military tracks suicide among service members but not among their family members, spouses, siblings, and parents. The Pentagon's Defense Suicide Prevention

134

Office has sent a report to Congress detailing for the first time a proposal for tracking those deaths.

The report came partly in response to cries for help from groups like the National Military Family Association, whose members know firsthand about the suicides and have struggled to call attention to the problem.

[32]The report says It would take 18 to 24 months for the Pentagon to analyze data it could buy from the Centers for Disease Control and Prevention's National Center for Health Statistics, which tracks deaths in the general U.S. population. That data — names and locations of deaths— could then be compared against data the Defense Department has on family members enrolled in an ID card program. The card allows them access to health benefits and other services, like shopping at on-base commissaries.

The cost of the effort, the report says was $681,600 the first year and $502,200 for each additional year.

"That amount is little to spend on something this important," said Kristina Kaufmann, a longtime military wife, who since 2006 has written editorials in national newspapers and spoken before Congress about the need to track military family member suicides. "A couple years ago, I had people telling me I was histrionic (attention seeking behavior and extreme emotionality). They'd say a bunch of military spouses weren't killing themselves. But we have the anecdotes. What we don't have is the actual data." [33]

Kaufmann personally knew military wives who committed suicide. She was a friend of Faye Vick. In 2006, the Fort Bragg mother placed her baby and two-year-old in the backseat of her car and asphyxiated them all.

Monique Lingenfelter was the wife of a sergeant assigned to a special operations unit at Bragg. In 2009, she barricaded herself in her home and shot herself.

The spouse of the highest-ranking military officer in the country tried to call attention to the problem four years ago. Deborah Mullen, wife of Adm. Mike Mullen, then the chairman of the Joint Chiefs of Staff, took the stage at a Defense Department conference to say she'd tried to get information about suicides among relatives. She met with leaders to see if they tracked such deaths by family members. Army leaders told her there were nine military family member suicides in 2009.

[34]Mullen said she asked Army officials if they knew how many family members had attempted suicide.

"I was stunned when I was told that there were too many to track," she told the crowd. "If that number is that large, just in the Army, we really don't have an idea of the scope of the problem."

"It's our responsibility," she implored. "These are our family members. We have got to find a way to track them."

An annual survey by Blue Star Families, the largest military family advocacy group, found suicide among relatives to be a critical concern. Out of 5,100 military family members interviewed in 2012, nine percent of military spouses reported that they had considered suicide. Of those, nearly a quarter said they had not sought help. [35]

Suicide in the military is a crisis, not just for those in the service, but also for family members. These men and women are sacrificing their lives and their families for our country. Why are so many getting poor wages? No one serving our country should have to be on food stamps. And family members should get all the support they need. The way we care for our military should be a top priority in this country

[36]**Veterans Crisis Line Website:** The Veterans Crisis Line connects veterans in crisis and their families and friends with qualified, caring Department of Veterans Affairs responders, through a confidential toll-free hotline, online chat, or text. Veterans and their loved ones can call 1-800-273-8255 and Press 1, to talk online.

Action Steps:

1. If you have been in the military and have post-traumatic stress, get help!
2. Don't pretend everything is OK when you are having nightmares and flashbacks. Get help!
3. Knock on doors and don't give up.
4. Get rid of weapons that could be used for suicide.

5. Tell your family and friends what you are going through, even if you think they won't understand. Get support.
6. Suicide is not an option!
7. Pouring out the rage on family members is not an acceptable option.
8. Go to your Veterans Hospital, talk to a Chaplain and get help.
9. If you can't get help from the military, go to your doctor and let him/her know what you are going through.
10. Don't give up - Get help!

A Reason To Live: The war is over. You are home, and yes, there are people who care about you. It is time to leave the war behind and live again.

16

Antidepressant Medications

Anti-depressants are a great aid to multitudes who deal with depression. But there are warnings on some medications that a side effect can be suicide or suicidal thoughts. When taking any drug, look at the side effects and if you experience any of them call your doctor immediately.

I was standing in line at the airport recently talking to the lady next to me. I told her I was writing a book on suicide. She said, "My best friend's fifteen-year-old son committed suicide."

"What happened," I asked.

"His mom took him to the doctor because he was a little depressed," she said. "The doctor put him on some medication that had a side effect of suicidal thoughts. He hung himself."

Teacher of the Year Commits Suicide

At our local high school, the man voted "Teacher of the Year" was prescribed some medication for depression. One of the side effects was suicidal thoughts and suicide. To everyone's shock, he killed himself leaving a wife and four daughters.

One of my close friend's sons, Jason, was put on medication for hyperactivity. We all knew he was not hyperactive. He would sit at a computer for hours playing games or doing homework. He's a genius in math and science. At the age of 14, he was going through some life changes that caused depression. A teenager often goes through life changes and losses that can cause depression. The doctor made a wrong diagnosis and put him on the wrong medicine. The medication he was put on caused more depression, and his thoughts became suicidal. He told his mother what he was feeling. She took him off the drug immediately and contacted the doctor. Jason began to feel better. He is 21 today and graduated at the top of his class in high school. Jason completed his first two years of college making straight A's. After watching the movie, "Gifted Hands," that tells of Dr. Ben Carson's life, he decided to become a doctor. He now works at a hospital while continuing his college education.

Medications Have Saved Many Lives

It is important to get on medication if you are dealing with clinical depression, schizophrenia, bipolar and/or other chemical imbalances. When going on any kind of new drug, it is important to notice side effects you may be having with them. If the prescription says that a side effect could be suicidal thoughts or suicide, make sure you call your doctor immediately if you are having suicidal thoughts. Tell family members about the side effects so they can look for signs. [37]

A New Class of Antidepressants Increase Risk of Suicide

SSRIs, (selective serotonin reuptake inhibitors), a relatively new class of antidepressants, have been associated with an increased chance of suicide. In tests of drugs of this type, on children with significant depressive disorders, about four percent of patients experienced suicidal thinking, behavior or attempts. In the placebo group, two percent of participants experienced similar problems. [38] If you or a loved one has been prescribed a SSRI type anti-depressant with a warning of suicidal thoughts, **please contact your doctor if you begin having thoughts of suicide.**

The warning also notes that children and adolescents taking SSRI medications should be monitored for any worsening in depression, the emergence of suicidal thinking or behavior, or unusual changes in behavior, such as sleeplessness, agitation, or withdrawal from normal social situations. Close monitoring is especially important during the first four weeks of treatment. SSRI medications usually have few side effects in children and adolescents, but for unknown reasons, they may trigger agitation and abnormal behavior in certain individuals.

More On SSRI's

"The antidepressant found in Robin Williams' toxicology test, (after his suicide), mirtazapine, (Remeron), has a warning about the possible thought of suicide.[39] You

141

should know that your mental health may change in unexpected ways when you take mirtazapine or other antidepressants even if you are an adult over 24 years of age. You may become suicidal, especially at the beginning of your treatment and any time that your dose is increased or decreased. You, your family, or your caregiver should call your doctor right away if you experience any of the following symptoms:

- New or worsening depression, thinking about harming or killing yourself, or planning or trying to do so.
- Extreme worry; agitation; panic attacks; difficulty falling asleep or staying asleep.
- Aggressive behavior; irritability or acting without thinking.
- Severe restlessness.
- Frenzied abnormal excitement.

Be sure that your family or caregiver knows which symptoms may be serious so they can call the doctor if you are unable to seek treatment on your own.

Your healthcare provider will want to see you often while you are taking mirtazapine, particularly in the beginning of your treatment. Be sure to keep all appointments for office visits with your doctor.

In response, the FDA adopted a **"Black Box"** label warning indicating that antidepressants may increase the risk of **suicidal thinking** and behavior in some children and adolescents with MDD, (Major depressive disorder). A black-box warning is the most serious type of warning in prescription drug labeling.

In addition to suicidal thoughts, documented side effects of antidepressants by international drug regulatory agencies include hallucinations, delusions, worsening depression, depersonalization, mania, psychosis, self-harm.

Action Steps When Taking Medications

1. Keep a diary of the reactions you are having when using a new medicine.
2. If you are getting dark, depressing, suicidal feelings talk to your doctor and those closest to you.
3. Be persistent in keeping your doctor informed on how the medication is affecting you.
4. Get rid of all guns, other weapons or medications you are tempted to overdose with and give them to someone you trust.

A Reason To Live: I can do all things through Christ who guides, directs and empowers me. Although the dark clouds of depression surround me, just beyond the clouds, the sun still shines. I have a reason to live.

17

Suicide Intervention

When God Intervenes

God often intervenes when a person who is ready to commit suicide, calls on Him for help. In the following story, God involved Himself in this man's life.

On a Saturday night several weeks ago, a minister was working late and decided to call his wife before he left for home. It was about 10:00 pm, but his wife didn't answer the phone.

The pastor let the phone ring many times. He thought it was odd that she didn't answer but decided to finish his work and try again in a few minutes. When he called again, she answered right away. He asked her why she hadn't answered before.

"The phone hasn't rung here," she said.

The following Monday, the pastor, received a call at the church office. The caller asked, "Why did you call me on Saturday night?"

The pastor couldn't figure out what the man was talking about. Then the man said, "It rang and rang, but I didn't answer."

The pastor remembered the call and apologized for bothering him, explaining that he'd intended to call his wife.

"That's, OK," said the man, "I was planning to commit suicide on Saturday night, but before I did, I prayed, 'God if you're there, and you don't want me to do this, show me a sign now.' At that moment, my phone started to ring. I looked at the caller ID, and it said, 'Almighty God.' I was afraid to answer!"

*The reason **"Almighty God"** showed on his answering machine is because the name of the church is **"Almighty God Tabernacle."***

Overcoming Depression By Thanksgiving and Praise

Samuel Logan Brengle, (a commissioner, author, and teacher in the Salvation Army), shares a way to overcome depression, "Prayer brought me no relief. Indeed, I seemed to have lost the spirit of prayer and the power to pray. Then I remembered to give thanks and to praise God though I felt no spirit of praise and thanksgiving. That feeling of utter depression and gloom was gone. As I thanked God for the trial, it began to turn to blessing; light glimmered, grew very slowly, and then broke through the gloom. The depression passed away, and life was beautiful and desirable again and full of gracious incomings once more."[40]

In my own battle with depression and suicidal thoughts, I have discovered that thanking God for what I have and praising Him can totally change my perspective on life. I had been sick and in bed for months while pregnant with my youngest daughter. In that dark time, I praised God for what I had; eyes that could see and read, ears that could hear, a mouth that could speak, a mind that could understand, a bed to rest in, legs that could walk, and hands that could type. As I praised Him, I began to feel strength return to my body. It was at that time that I started writing.

After her delivery I was in a postpartum depression so severe, it was nearly impossible to get out of bed. Each night before going to bed I would write down scriptures and put them beside the bed to meditate on before going to sleep and in the morning before getting up. One such scripture that helped me was; *"The Lord is my strength and my salvation."* (Ps.27:1)

Helping Alice Find Hope in the Midst of Her Husband's Affair

I called a friend, Alice late one morning. Her voice was monotone. I could feel the depression over the phone. "What's going on?" I asked.

"I have been lying here for three days trying to figure out how to end my life," Alice said. "I have pills lined up on my nightstand."

"Have you taken anything," I asked.

"No," she said in a slow and melancholy voice.

"I am on my way over to see you!" I told her.

Had there been cell phones at that time I would have kept her on the line until I got there. I knew I needed to get to her as quickly as I could.

When I arrived at the house, her husband was downstairs acting like nothing was wrong. "Your wife has been in bed for three days and you act like nothing is wrong," I said as I walked up the stairs.

Alice was in bed with the pills on the nightstand. "Get up and get dressed!" I said. "We are going to a coffee shop to talk."

She got up and put on a beautiful dress and fixed her hair and makeup. She was a very attractive, educated woman. We drove over to a little café where we sat, talked, drank hot chocolate and discussed her husband's affair. We talked for hours about the shock and grief of knowing her marriage was over. By the end of the conversation, she had made up her mind to live, rather than die. I helped her make a plan to go to counseling and take some time off to enjoy life. We talked about going on a vacation to the mountains with her 10-year-old daughter. She prepared a plan to face the future without her husband. She had always wanted to live in California. She decided to move to there once the divorce was final. She did move to California with her daughter and later married again.

How to Help Someone That is Suicidal

The following is a list of ways to help someone who is suicidal. As I drove to help Alice, I prayed for God to give me wisdom. I have never sought to help someone choose life, without first praying for God's assistance. Psychologists have put together formulas of how to help

147

someone who is suicidal. They may help to an extent, but what is most important is to PRAY and LISTEN.

- When talking to someone that is suicidal, don't be afraid to ask if they are thinking about suicide.
- Listen and take what they are saying seriously.
- Help them look at other options. Feelings of self-hate, hopelessness, emotional pain and isolation make it difficult for the suicidal person to see any relief except through death. Most suicidal people do not really want to end their lives. They just can't see any way out except suicide
- Let them know you care and are there for them.
- Be a safe person for them to talk to. Be sympathetic, non-judgmental, calm and accepting.
- Don't tell them what to do or give a lot of advice. Instead, ask open questions and help them to see there are other options – better ones.
- If they have a weapon or source they plan to use to kill themselves, get it away from them. Get the person into a different environment. If they have a gun, razor or knife, they refuse to give up, stay calm and attempt to talk them out of it. You may need to call 911. Don't use the call as a threat, but rather as a way to get more help for them. Stay calm, strong, and wise for your friend in crisis.
- In some cases having them sign a contract with you helps prevent suicide.
- Do not swear secrecy when someone's life is at stake.

- See that the person finds assistance.
- If they are in a dark room or bedroom, have them go to a public place to talk.
- If the person has not eaten or had anything to drink, get them to eat something.
- Do not leave the person if he or she expresses a plan as to how they will commit suicide.
- Do not let the person alone if they are in a confused or in a manic state and talking about killing themselves.
- If they are in a manic state, hear voices or see visions, encourage them to go to the hospital or call an ambulance. They may need to get on medication. If they refuse to go to the hospital, do not leave them. Call someone they trust to assist you. Read How We Helped David (Bipolar) "Not to Commit Suicide," Chapter 8.
- Call the Suicide Help Line-1-800-SUICIDE or `1-800-783-2483

A Reason To Live: God has a plan for your life. Today's sorrows are tomorrow's blessings.

18

Overcoming Suicidal Thoughts

You Are God's Gift to the World

"You think you are God's gift to the world," I heard my mother's angry voice say when I was a child.

Years later, as an adult, those words went through my mind. The Holy Spirit within me broke the curse saying, *"You ARE MY gift to the world!"*

Only God has the right to say who we are. People define us by who they are or by what we can give to them. God has created us to fulfill His purpose, and He knows who we are.

At the age of 24, I had gone through a difficult pregnancy and surgery. Every day was a struggle for me to find the strength even to get out of bed. Weak and broken I remember God speaking to my spirit saying, *"You are my princess, my bride, my beloved."*

I pondered the thought, "How could a mess like me be a princess of the almighty God? Well, I am a child of God.

That makes me a princess. How would she act? How would she look?"

I went into the bathroom and fixed my hair and put on a little make-up. "Since I am a princess, I will seek to look and act like one," I told myself.

My dear friend; it is no accident that you are reading this. You are a part of God's kingdom. He has a plan for your life. His plan for you is not suicide but a life full of love, joy, and peace. No matter what others have said about you or to you, **God loves you**. You are His gift to the world.

"SUICIDE IS NOT AN OPTION" - Under no circumstance is suicide the way out of emotional or physical pain. You do not want to leave a legacy of "Suicide."

You Become What You Think

You become what you think about. If you think negative thoughts about your life, you will become depressed. Thoughts of suicide can eventually end up as an action. If you think all day about divorce, death, and suicide, you are most likely going to end up in the pit of despair. Our thoughts come from the people we are around, our past, what we read, what we feed our minds and at times from evil spirits. The Bible says, *"For we are not fighting against flesh-and-blood enemies, but against evil rulers and authorities of the unseen world, against mighty powers in this dark world, and against evil spirits in the heavenly places."* (Eph. 6:12 NLT)

151

A key to overcoming negative thoughts is to invite the Holy Spirit to live in your heart and pray that Christ will fill your mind with His thoughts. *"He that is within you is greater than he that is in the world."* (I John 4:4) How do you know if an evil spirit is influencing you? Accusations, condemnation, hopelessness and self-hate are techniques used by Satan to destroy and discourage us. We need to put every thought under subjection to the Lord Jesus Christ. What kind of things do you think about all day long? "I'm stupid. I can't do anything right. I wish I were dead." These don't come from God but from our adversary, the devil.

Thoughts can heal or destroy. You can change your thought life. Suicide and depression are not your answer. No matter how rejected, hated, controlled or bullied you have been, God has a great plan for your life. He loves you with an everlasting love. You are special to Him. He is willing to listen to the way you feel and will help you. Don't give up. **God loves you!**

New Life-New Beginning

What can you do? Let the Lord Jesus Christ take over and fill your mind with His thoughts.

When Adam and Eve sinned in the Garden after eating of the tree of the knowledge of "Good and Evil," sin came into the world. They already had the knowledge of **Good**. All they had to gain was the knowledge of evil. They were then put out of the garden because God did not want them to eat of the "Tree of Life." If they had eaten from the Tree of Life, they would have lived forever, in a state of sin.

Since Christ has come into the world, laying down His life as a sacrifice for our sins, we may now eat of the "Tree of Life." Jesus is the "Tree of Life!" Some years ago I had a dream. I stood at the gate of the Garden of Eden. I heard a voice from inside the garden which said, "You may come into the Garden now."

I said, "We have been put out of the Garden because of our sin."

Then I heard a voice from inside the Garden say, *"Father, forgive her for she knew not what she was doing."*

Since Jesus is the "Tree of Life" when we accept Jesus as our Lord and Savior, we have eaten of the Real Tree. He said at the last supper, *"This is my body, given for you. This cup is the new covenant written in my blood, blood poured out for you.* (Matt. 26:26-29)

When we eat the Lord's Supper, we are eating from the "Tree of Life" through the body and blood of Jesus. When we give our lives to Jesus, we become a part of Him. He says, *"I am the vine; you are the branches. If you remain in me and I in you, you will bear much fruit; apart from me you can do nothing."* (John 15:5)

All of us have sinned and fallen short of what God's plan is for us. But when we commit our lives to Christ we are born again spiritually. We receive a new spirit. The Spirit

153

of God within us. All our past failures are forgotten, and we begin anew, with the new Spirit. We are given the power to say "**No**" to evil and "**Yes** to God.

Living in an Imperfect World

We continue to live in an imperfect world with cruelty, hatred, war and destructive forces coming at us daily. The scriptures tell us that we are to be in the world, but not of it. *"In the world, we will have tribulation, but take heart, I [Christ] have overcome the world."* (John 6:33)

If our expectations are perfection, we will always be disappointed with others, the world, and ourselves. What we need to know is although we live in an imperfect world; God is within us forgiving and empowering us through it all.

Thoughts That Heal, Renew and Give Hope

The Apostle Paul knew better than most what it was like to live in the world, but not to be a part of it. After his encounter with Jesus, he became a strong Christian whose mission was to bring as many as he could, to understand and know Christ.

He was in prison after being stoned when he wrote the following words; *"Always be full of joy in the Lord. I say it again—rejoice! Let everyone see that you are considerate in all you do. Remember, the Lord is coming soon. Don't worry about anything; instead, pray about everything. Tell God what you need, and thank him for all*

154

he has done. Then you will experience God's peace, which exceeds anything we can understand. His peace will guard your hearts and minds as you live in Christ Jesus. And now, dear brothers and sisters, one final thing. Fix your thoughts on what is true, and honorable, and right, and pure, and lovely, and admirable. Think about things that are excellent and worthy of praise." (Phil. 4:4-8 NLT)

If there was ever a prescription for joy and hope it is to pray about everything, look for the good and rejoice. Knowing Paul was in prison when he wrote this gives us no excuse not to pray, think of the good and praise God. The power of Satan's accusations, negative thoughts and death cannot live in a heart filled with praise and thanksgiving.

God Will Provide – Don't Worry

He tells us not to worry and has promised to take care of all our needs. *"My God will meet all your needs according to the riches of his glory in Christ Jesus."* (Phil. 4:19)

After the birth of our youngest daughter, we had bills we could not pay and a new baby. We were behind on our house payments. I feared we would lose our home. I was overwhelmed and had no idea what to do. I poured my heart out to God and prayed for a miracle. In my mind, I heard these words, **"I own the cattle on a thousand hills, and I can pay your bills."**

The phone rang later that day. A lady from church asked, "How much do you owe in back house payments?" I told her, and she wrote a check and sent it to the mortgage company. God owns everything; He cares for the sparrows and the weeds in the field. Think how much more He cares about you and me and is able to meet all our needs – we just have to ask Him. Suicide was not an option. **Prayer was!**

We Are Not Perfect

Because we live in the world, our bodies are not perfect. Many have chemical imbalances that need medication. Just as a diabetic needs insulin, many need medications for bi-polar, schizophrenia, depression and other chemical imbalances in the body. If you are dealing with an imbalance in the body, you need to get medical care. When you are given a new medication, read the warnings and side effects. Contact your doctor if you experience any that concern you. Some anti-depressants may cause suicidal thoughts. If this occurs, contact your physician immediately.

When Medication is Needed

Years ago when I wrote a column called, *Inspiration Point*, for local newspapers, one of the churches called asking if I could help one of their members. James, a 30-year-old man, had come to them asking for prayer saying the devil was biting and attacking him. I met with him and his mother at a local restaurant. He and I sat down to talk while his mother waited outside. All of a sudden he began hitting himself and yelling, "He's biting me. The devil is biting me all over."

Waitresses started surrounding us, as I calmly told him that it was not the devil. I said, "James, you have a chemical imbalance in your body, and we need to get you to the hospital. They will be able to put you on some medicine so you won't feel this anymore."

James and his mother followed me in their car to the hospital. He checked himself in, and I told him I would come the next day to see how he was doing. When I arrived the next morning, he sat calmly on the edge of the bed and said, "You were right. All I needed was some medicine."

God has sent us doctors and medications to take care of many illnesses and imbalances in our bodies.

19

Search for Perfection

Battle with Evil

To a "cutter," (someone who cuts their body with some sharp instrument), physical pain is better than mental pain or no feelings at all. Although we live in a prosperous country, multitudes still suffer mental anguish. *"We fight not flesh and blood, but against powers and principalities, spirits without bodies. Evil rulers in the unseen world "* says the Bible in Ephesians 6:12. That is we fight against mighty satanic beings and evil princes of darkness who seek to rule the world and our lives with huge numbers of wicked spirits in the spirit world.

We can be free from the torture of mental pain. God has told us that if we give our lives to Him, He will fill us with the Holy Spirit, which is the Spirit of love, joy, and peace. One cannot see a soul, yet that pain can be greater than physical pain. It can come in the form of depression, fear, anger, and despair. It is expressed in behaviors such as cutting, suicide, and addictions. How can the mental tortures of hell in our soul be turned to love, joy and peace? God wants to fill us with His Spirit. All you need to do is ask. **Example**: "God, I give myself to you. I want Jesus to take over my life, and I ask that you fill me with your Holy

Spirit. Lead, guide and help me in the name of your Son Jesus."

Our Ideas of *Perfect*

Is "perfect" having an absolutely clean, organized house? Is "perfect" having healthy tasty meals on the table every night? Is "perfect" being a size two? Young girls are dying today because they refuse to eat. They think perfection is being a size two. Is it how much money we have, what kind of car we drive or the clothes we wear? Is perfection being muscular and vigorous? **What is "perfect"?** If I had a thoroughly clean house, yard, and garage but had no time to be with my children, it would all be foolishness. If my hair looked and smelled great, my body young, vigorous and beautiful but didn't love others, it would be nothing more than wood, hay, and stubble. Today we are bombarded with articles, books, programs and voices from every direction, telling us how to be perfect. We are told how to think, look, feel, eat, exercise, relax, work and live. There are thousands of beauty products to make us smell and look good. From the time we are very young, we are told in a hundred ways how to *be perfect*. "Don't say that, don't think that, don't feel that, don't look that way, don't make that noise, and …....."

Jesus had some special friends that he spent time with: Mary, Martha, and Lazarus. Martha was busy cleaning and getting food ready for Jesus. Mary was sitting at Jesus' feet listening to everything He had to say, and Martha got upset with Mary and told Jesus, *"Sir, doesn't it seem unfair to you that my*

159

sister just sits here while I do all the work? Tell her to come and help me."

"Martha, you are so upset over all these details!" Jesus said. *"There is really only one thing worth being concerned about. Mary has discovered it—and I won't take it away from her!"* (Luke 10:39-42)

I think that is an example of what is important to God. We worry about so many things, but what is most important? I have never heard a woman say at the end of her life, "I wish I had spent more time cleaning." I have never listened to a man say at the end of his life, "I wish I had spent more time at the office." But I have heard, "I wish I had gone with the kids and their dad to the park and spent less time cleaning."

What I see as perfect is getting to know Jesus and loving others. Honor God first, and He will help you take care of the rest. Love others first, and God will help you take care of what is really most important. Our drive for perfection can keep us from loving God, others and ourselves.

After I had given birth to my youngest child, I felt depressed because I could not maintain a clean and organized house. God showed me what was most important was to love my baby and those He put in my care. This meant spending time with them.

What Is Perfect to God

What is perfect? The only perfection that has ever walked the face of this earth is Jesus Christ, who is described in Isaiah 53. Isaiah was a prophet that lived 740 years before Christ. What you are reading here is a prophecy of what Jesus would do and be like when he came over 700 years later. ***There was nothing beautiful or majestic about his appearance, nothing to attract us to him.***

We all think we have to be beautiful or handsome to be perfect. Jesus didn't come as one who was attractive. Women didn't turn their heads to look at Him because there was nothing physically attractive about Him to make them take a second look. (Isa. 53:3-12 NIV)

> *He was despised and rejected by mankind,*
> *A man of suffering, and familiar with pain.*
> *Like one from whom people hide their faces*
> *He was despised, and we held him in low esteem.*

No one was bullied more than Jesus Christ. Yet, He healed the brokenhearted and set the captive free. He opened the eyes of the blind. Often when I look at people whom, God uses in marvelous ways, it is those who are not perfect by our standards. Corrie Ten Boom was not physically beautiful. She was called the "double old grandmother" by those in Vietnam, whom she served. She survived a Nazi Concentration Camp to spend her life helping others who suffered. She helped multitudes find hope.

> *Surely he took up our pain*
> *And bore our suffering,*
> *yet we considered him punished by God,*

161

stricken by him, and afflicted. But he was pierced for our transgressions,
he was crushed for our iniquities;
The punishment that brought us peace was upon him, and by his wounds, we are healed. We all, like sheep, have gone astray,
each of us has turned to our own way;
*and the L*ORD *has laid on him*
the iniquity of us all.

He was oppressed and afflicted,
yet he did not open his mouth;
He was led like a lamb to the slaughter,
and as a sheep before its shearers is silent,
so he did not open his mouth. By oppression and judgment, he was taken away.
Yet who of his generation protested?
For he was cut off from the land of the living;
for the transgression of my people he was punished[j]

He was assigned a grave with the wicked,
and with the rich in his death
though he had done no violence,
nor was any deceit in his mouth.

[10] *Yet it was the L*ORD*'s will to crush him and cause him to suffer,*
*and though the L*ORD *makes his life an offering for sin, he will see his offspring and prolong his days,*
*and the will of the L*ORD *will prosper in his hand.*
After he has suffered, he will see the light of life and be satisfied;
by his knowledge, my righteous servant will justify many, and he will bear their iniquities.

Therefore, I will give him a portion among the great
and he will divide the spoils with the strong
because he poured out his life unto death
and was numbered with the transgressors.
For he bore the sin of many
and made intercession for the transgressors.

Jesus was not recognized as perfect at the time. The world thought perfect would be rich, powerful, strong, handsome and famous. Instead, God's definition of perfect was humble, poor, and simple. Yet because of His love and sacrifice for others, (and of course His sinlessness) He is counted as perfect. He was fully human and fully God in the flesh. And because of His sacrifice, we will live forever with Him. He said, "*I am the resurrection and the life. He who believes in me shall never die.*" (John 11:25)

20

Myths and Truths About Suicide

There are many false beliefs, (myths) that are dangerous in the prevention of suicide. To know what is *Truth* and what is *Myth* may help you keep yourself or someone else from making that fatal decision. If you are depressed and suicidal, you need to know the truth.

- **Myth**: Real Christians do not experience suicidal thoughts.
- **Truth:** Christians live in broken bodies in a world that is not perfect. Today I spoke to a Christian women's group about this book. One of the ladies said she deals with suicidal thoughts all the time because of the medication she takes for seizures.
- **Myth**: People who kill themselves are selfish.
- **Truth:** People who take their own lives are in pain.
- **Myth**: People who talk about suicide won't really do it.
- **Truth:** Most who have attempted or completed suicide have given some kind of warning. Do not ignore suicide threats!

- **Myth**: Anyone who tries to kill themselves is crazy.
- **Truth:** People who attempt suicide are not necessarily insane. They are upset, grief-stricken, depressed, fearful, overwhelmed or in despair. Emotional pain is usually not a sign of mental illness.
- **Myth:** All people who try to commit suicide really want to die.
- **Truth:** Many who are suicidal have mixed feelings. Often they do not desire to die; they just want to end the pain.
- **Myth**: Suicide can't be prevented. If someone decides to kill themselves, nothing can stop them.
- **Truth:** Suicide is preventable. The majority of people thinking about suicide don't actually want to die. They are seeking to end mental and/or physical pain. Interventions can save lives.
- **Myth**: People who commit suicide are unwilling to seek help
- **Truth:** More than half the people who commit suicide have sought medical or other types of help within six months before their death.
- **Myth**: People who take their own life are cowards, weak or looking for attention.
- **Truth:** More than ninety percent of those who take their own life have at least one and often more than one treatable condition such as depression, borderline personality, seasonal affect disorder, anxiety, bipolar disorder, schizophrenia, postpartum

depression, and/or alcohol and substance abuse. With better recognition and treatment, many suicides could be prevented.

- **Myth:** Asking someone if they are thinking about suicide will plant that idea in their head and cause them to act on it.
- **Truth:** When you fear someone you know is in crisis or depressed, asking them if they are thinking about suicide can actually help; it is one of the most helpful things you can do for them. By giving a person an opportunity to open up and share their troubles you can often help alleviate their pain and find solutions
- **Myth**: Barriers on bridges, safe firearm storage and other actions to reduce access to lethal methods of suicide don't work. People will just find another way.
- **Truth:** Limiting access to lethal methods of suicide is one of the best strategies for suicide prevention. Many suicides can be impulsive and triggered by an immediate crisis. Separating someone in crisis from a lethal method such as guns can give them something they desperately need: time. Time to change their mind, time to resolve the crisis, time for someone to intervene.
- **Myth**: Talk therapy and/or medications don't work.
- **Truth:** This is incredibly *FALSE*. Sometimes all it takes to save a life is an anti-depressant. Treatment can work! One of the best ways to prevent suicide is by getting treatment for depression, bipolar

disorder, seasonal affect disorder, borderline personality and/or substance abuse and learning ways to solve problems. Treatment can significantly reduce the risk of suicide.

Other Truths about Suicide

- [41]**Truth:** White males over the age of 85 have a suicide rate of 49.8 deaths per 100,000, compared with about 14 per 100,000 in people over 65, and 11 per 100,000 in the general population.
- **Truth:** Suicide attempts are **more** common than AIDS, cancer, and diabetes combined. More than 400,000 people attempt suicide in the U.S. every year.
- **Truth:** Though depression and suicide are common and dangerous problems, many people don't know that much about them, including who's at the greatest risk, why, and when they are most likely to be vulnerable.
- **Truth:** Whites attempt suicide more often than other races. Suicide is more common among whites in the U.S. than Blacks, Asians, or Hispanics.
- **Truth:** The only group at higher risk than Whites is Native Americans and Alaskan Natives, who have a suicide rate of 14.3 per 100,000 compared to 13.5 per 100,000 for whites and about 5 to 6 per 100,000 for other groups.

- [42]**Truth:** Creativity, depression, and suicide have long been linked so it may come as no surprise that some of the most creative individuals in history have suffered from depression. It affected great minds such as Charles Dickens, John Keats, and Tennessee Williams, to name just a few. As I looked at the childhood of these three men, I saw trauma in each of their lives. Dickens father was put in debtor prison. As a child, he lived in extreme poverty which gave him the background and compassion to write. Dickens childhood as a child laborer inspired his book Oliver Twist, where he wrote about child labor, street children and recruiting children as criminals. John Keats father died when he was eight, and his mother died when he was fourteen. Because doctors feared he would commit suicide, they would not give Keats opium even at the end of his life while suffering from tuberculosis. Keats died at the age of 25. Although he inherited a lot of money when turning 21, he was not told of his inheritance. He suffered financially throughout his life. Tennessee Williams was a fragile child suffering from diphtheria which nearly took his life. His father had a violent temper and was disgusted with his son's physical weakness.

In researching the lives of incredibly creative people who have suffered from depression, I often see traumatic childhoods.

Endnotes

Chapter 4

[1] http://www.huffingtonpost.com/2013/04/06/matthew-warren-suicide_n_3029792.html

[2] Kay Warren on YouTube presentation – "Walking Through Catastrophic Grief"

[3] ibid

Chapter 5

[4] http://www.angelfire.com/ok2/tellnow/facts.html

[5] http://www.angelfire.com/ok2/tellnow/facts.html

[6] http://www.angelfire.com/ok2/tellnow/facts.html

Chapter 8

[7] National Institute of Mental Health

[8] ibid

[9] World Health Organization

[10] National Institute of Mental Health

[11] Birmaher, B., "Childhood and Adolescent Depression: A Review of the Past 10 Years."1995

[12] American Academy of Child and Adolescent Psychiatry, 1997

[13] National Institute of Mental Health

[14] Bipolar Disorder Statistics - (DBSA, 2000)

Chapter 10

[15] Feeling Good: The New Mood Therapy by David D. Burns

[16] Joni, by Joni Eareckson Tada, pg. 1-5, Inspiration Press

Chapter 12

[17] http://abcnews.go.com/US/teen-charged-fatal-cyberbullying-case-rebecca-sedwick-emain/story?id=20580689

Chapter 13

[18] http://www.huffingtonpost.com/2010/07/06/high-college-suicide-rate_n_636878.html

Chapter 14

[19] http://kdvr.com/2013/10/30/2-freshmen-reported-dead-in-csu-dorms-in-past-2-weeks/
[20] People of the Lie, by Scott Peck, MD pgs. 56-57
[21] ibid
[22] http://godlovesyou-adron.blogspot.com/2011/03/what-is-evil-according-to-bible.html

Chapter 15

[23] *http://billygraham.org/answer/my-sister-struggled-with-severe-depression-most-of-her-life-and-had-to-be-hospitalized-several-times-last-year-she-finally-got-so-depressed-that-she-took-her-own-life-in-spite-of-everything-she-ha/*
[24] http://billygraham.org/answer/is-suicide-the-unpardonable /
[25] Preventing Suicide, by Karen Mason
[26] http://maxlucado.com/faqs/a-close-relative-recently-committed-suicide-does-max-have-any-writings-on-this-that-would-help-give-our-family-some-peace-of-mind/
[27] http://thinkingaboutsuicide.com/max-lucado-shares-words-of-hope-to-depressed-and-suicidal/

Chapter 16

[28] http://www.donnelly.senate.gov/issues/preventsuicide
[29] http://www.fra.org/AM/template.cfm?ContentID=13039&template=/CM/ContentDisplay.cfm
[30] http://abcnews.go.com/Health/vietnam-vets-highest-rates-suicide-alongisde-baby-boomers/story?id=19100593
[31] http://www.cnn.com/2014/02/05/us/military-family-suicides/
[32] ibid

[33] ibid

[34] ibid

[35] https://www.bluestarfam.org/news/releases/blue-star-families-fifth-annual-military-family-lifestyle-survey-shows-effects-13

[36] http://veteranscrisisline.net/

Chapter 17

[37] http://www.nimh.nih.gov/health/topics/child-and-adolescent-mental-health/antidepressant-medications-for-children-and-adolescents-information-for-parents-and-caregivers.shtml

[38] http://www.drugwatch.com/ssri/suicide/

[39]

http://www.fda.gov/Drugs/DrugSafety/InformationbyDrugClass/ucm096273.htm

Chapter 18

[40] Brengle, *Heart Talks On Holiness*

Chapter 21

[41] https://www.yahoo.com/health/15-myths-and-facts-about-suicide-and-depression-94537114763.html

[42] ibid

www.ingramcontent.com/pod-product-compliance
Lightning Source LLC
LaVergne TN
LVHW051058080426
835508LV00019B/1941